THE ART INSTITUTE OF PORTLAND

Reinventing Music Video

D0896198

Next-generation directors,

their inspiration and work

MATT HANSON

ELSEVIER

Amsterdam · Boston · Heidelberg · London
New York · Oxford · Paris · San Diego
San Francisco · Singapore · Sydney · Tokyo
Focal Press is an imprint of Elsevier

Focal Press

24 DIGITAL-AGE MUSIC VIDEO: THE DIRECTORS

26

ADAM LEVITE
(AKA ASSOCIATES
IN SCIENCE)

36

BESSY & COMBE

44

BRAND NEW SCHOOL

84

HIDEAKI MOTOKI

92

MUTO MASASHI

100

ne-o

142

RAMON & PEDRO

152

VERNIE YEUNG

160

WOOF WAN-BAU

 **52** BEN DAWKINS

 **62** MARTIN DE THURAH

 **74** CHRIS MILK

 **108** PLEIX

 **120** JONAS ODELL

 **128** +cruz

 # FOREWORD

Dire Straits' *Money for Nothing* video had an indelible impact on me. The first video shown at the launch of MTV Europe in 1987, it featured cutting-edge graphics, laughably crude by modern standards, but absolutely up to the minute at the time. It still retains a charm, and an afterglow of modernity even now for me.

Personally, therefore, I find music video is quite an intimate thing. I think it is also an intimate form. I've tried to reflect that in my more personal impressions of the work, and the same in terms of how each director's emerging oeuvre make me feel. I hope these recollections make the book feel less academic and elicit a more emotional response in the reader.

Each director was kind enough to make themselves available, so each section contains an all-new, completely original interview with them that I believe communicates hints of insight and personality missing from any straight reading or industry rendition of their work. The book also presents a kaleidoscopic range of styles, an array of different approaches that is both dizzying and breathtaking.

I can't believe music video isn't a more studied area, because the work captured within these pages is awe-inspiring. And currently the form stands in a tremendously exciting time—with the advent of the video-enabled iPod, the PSP, and other portable video playback devices, music video is going through a transitional time of upheaval and mayhem—always nice to watch.

This period also presents a changing of the guard. Something that has been at the crux of this book's creation. There has been a tremendous influx of new talent into the industry arena, and this book reflects that. Familiar names are moving on to feature formats, keeping their hand in with a video or two here or there.

I hope this book illuminates and gets you fired up about the medium. I hope it makes you want to see more videos. The best thing people have ever said to me about my work is that I gave them something that filled them with inspiration. I hope this book offers some of that—reviewing the directors' work for this project did just that for me.

Matt Hanson

Next spread:
Yamono, Hifana. by +cruz

FADE IN:
THE IMPORTANCE OF MUSIC VIDEO

Music video is a perfectly formed, contemporary moving image form: Quintessentially based on reinvention, reimagining, never standing still; always looking different; being in flux; moving. What is in vogue this year should be completely different from the last. One minute, it's clean lines, vector graphics, and silhouettes; the next, stop motion with Fuzzy Felt, Lego bricks, and old cards. The frame can't freeze.

Music video stands in a uniquely important position. It acts as a confluence point for the more freeform moving image arts. It provides a place where visual and narrative experiments can be distilled into a populist short form. And, increasingly, it has become a bridge between these younger forms and the dominant, more formal cinematic disciplines. It inhabits that crucial space between the commercial and the experimental, and acts as the crossover point.

Is it heresy to suggest that modern film would be nowhere without the music video? It would definitely be less interesting. So it is ironic that it has been so derided, scoffed at by those untuned to what was once called "MTV culture" (read: modern culture.)

Why do I like music videos so much? Because they offer up, in their flash cuts and whip pans, glimpses of filmmaking futures. Music video, in its populist way, pollutes the still waters of cinematic grammar. And the most exciting filmmakers shaking up genres, burning up celluloid, are from this (un)discipline: Spike Jonze, Michel Gondry, Jonathan Glazer—only the latest music video alumni who have received Academy Award recognition for their debutante feature film efforts—are talents that attest to what I have previously described, in *The End of Celluloid* [1] as "accelerated cinema." This is a cinema where ideas, both visual and conceptual, hit you thick and fast.

We have travelled beyond "cinema lite." The pop promo is more than a mere training ground for directors on their way to the extended form. Pre-desktop digital video, the music promo aspired to be mini-movie. It borrowed from the most influential films to create a post-modern medium. The digital age has seen this assimilation spread to every visual art. The best videos can appropriate myriad animated styles from 3D, motion graphics, computer gaming, and VJing to vivid effect. Yet these videos can also be simplistic, stark visual haiku—bringing forth the essences of things, tracing wondrously pure forms.

Music video has become meta-cinema. With the proliferation of digital television, channels concentrating on different music genres, and our online viewing of the medium exploding, the audience has never been more enraptured by the forms' exuberant visual sampling and remixing of ideas. Its directors can no longer be dismissed as arch stylists, as mere exponents of the intricate art of trucage (trick photography), as they are also demonstrably innovative with narrative structure, with the mise-en-scène.

Music video is a place where the moving image avant-garde comes alive, where it is translated into a universal language. A place where, once more, we can be blinded by the light.

Source:
[1] *The End of Celluloid*, Matt Hanson (RotoVision, 2004)

FLASH CUTS, WHIP PANS: A SNAPSHOT HISTORY OF THE MUSIC VIDEO

Year	Director	Video	Artist/Band	Comment
1949	Oskar Fischinger	*Motion Painting No. 1*		Won the Grand Prix at the Brussels International Experimental Film Competition.
1964	Richard Lester	*A Hard Day's Night*	The Beatles	The feature film that helped define the visual grammar of music video.
1966	DA Pennebaker	*Subterranean Homesick Blues*	Bob Dylan	The famous cue cards held by Dylan in DA Pennebaker's video suggested music video's future graphic explorations.
1967	Peter Goldman	*Strawberry Fields Forever*	The Beatles	Early model of more conceptual music videos, with less reportage or performance-based filming.
1968	Norman McLaren	*Pas de Deux*		Used groundbreaking visual effects and layering techniques.
1975	Bruce Gowers	*Bohemian Rhapsody*	Queen	Landmark video that heralded the arrival of the modern pop video.
1980	Gerald V Casale	*Whip It!*	Devo	Music video indulging in post-modern bricolage, hinting at a more subversive art form.
1981	Godley & Creme	*Girls on Film*	Duran Duran	Highly-influential epitome of the "lifestyle" music video projecting a band's glamorous image.
1981	William Dear	*Elephant Parts*	Michael Nesmith	The first video album and first winner of a Grammy for music video.
1983	Steve Barron	*Billie Jean*	Michael Jackson	Featuring a black dance act, *Billie Jean* redefined the direction of MTV and music video at the time.
1984	John Landis	*Thriller*	Michael Jackson	The first blockbuster music video, *Thriller* had the production costs and values of a miniature film.
1985	Steve Barron	*Take on Me*	a-ha	Morten Harket's transformation from real to drawn character is a prime example of music video's pioneering role in the development of animation/live action hybrids.
1988	Robert Breer & William Wegman	*Blue Monday 88*	New Order	Music video meets the worlds of modern art and photography.
1990	Jean-Baptiste Mondino	*Justify My Love*	Madonna	The fashion world collides with music video.

FREEZE-FRAME:
ICONS OF
THE GENRE

It was first thought that the perceptual processes of the brain, the retina of the human eye, retains an image for a split second. This is the theory of persistence of vision, that has permeated through established film theory. Then we had "phi phenomenon," an explanation of filmic motion that goes beyond this original notion, which asserted that the spaces between the frames didn't exist because of flicker fusion, and "apparent motion," created by a succession of film or video images. Some modern theories [1] expound that we have moved even further beyond this understanding, and that the motion we actually process in a motion picture is perceived and processed in the same way as it is in the real world. To the eye, it is therefore indistinguishable from reality, the "motion" we experience all around us.

Why all the theory? Because, if this is the case, then the motion pieces created by this select set of music video directors have, for countless individuals, redefined their reality. Even if there is no such thing as persistence of vision, then those of us who love watching music video, when we shut our eyes and think of a specific moment or emotion, recall in a freeze-frame or particular shot—a movement—the work of some of these directors. This is not a definitive list, but a collection that forms part of my personal canon.

The following directors are often cited by the filmmakers I have interviewed throughout this book as major influencers or inspirations for their own work. They all happen to be directors who have helped redefine the genre. They are the ones who have created the music video clips the next generation aspire to. The powerful, the emotional, the ecstatic.

Source:
[1] *The Myth of Persistence of Vision Revisited*, Joseph and Barbara Anderson; *Journal of Film and Video*, Vol. 45, No. 1 (Spring 1993): 3-12.

CHRIS CUNNINGHAM

- **ALL IS FULL OF LOVE**
- ► **BJÖRK**

- **COME TO DADDY**
- ► **APHEX TWIN**

Cunningham's work presents us with the agony and the ecstacy—it feeds on the extremes of cinematic shorthand. *All is Full of Love* presents a paean to technology as a robotic Björk is built before our eyes, the songstress reimagined in ceramic, white, cybernetic form. Cunningham's biomechanical love story imbues the erotic into the artificial.

Come to Daddy, meanwhile, is in direct contrast: A dirtier vision, distilling carefully selected motifs of the horror form as a miniature "end of days" on an English housing estate. Menacing prepubescent clones run amok, sporting the grotesquely warped features of Richard D. James (Aphex Twin). I read it as a scream against urban decay.

(01) *All is Full of Love*, Björk
(02) *Come to Daddy*, Aphex Twin

(02)

(01)

JONATHAN GLAZER

■ A RABBIT IN YOUR HEADLIGHTS
▶ UNKLE FEATURING THOM YORKE

■ STREET SPIRIT
▶ RADIOHEAD

Two videos of immense emotional power that both center around a number of shots filmed in exquisite slow motion. Set in an American trailer park somewhere "East of LA," *Street Spirit* is the epitomy of a waking dream. Elements move at different speeds within the same shot while barking dogs, a cricket, the band members, are engulfed in a monochromatic visual. A surreal trap of absence, they wait—*kill* time—for something extraordinary to happen.

That thing they might be waiting for, that is the thing that actually happens in the grittier, intense, UNKLE video for *A Rabbit in Your Headlights*. A crazed pedestrian bisects a busy underground road. Walking through it, he is constantly buffeted by passing cars. Reeling, he looks set to be crushed by an oncoming automobile when, through an act of transubstantiation, he presents himself Christ-like, arms held apart, against the traffic. The hard metal crumples against his fragile human form.

[02]

(01) *Street Spirit*, Radiohead
(02) *A Rabbit in Your Headlights*, UNKLE

MICHEL GONDRY

- **FELL IN LOVE WITH A GIRL**
▶ **THE WHITE STRIPES**

- **AROUND THE WORLD**
▶ **DAFT PUNK**

Through temporal shifts and stylistic, often prop-based elements, Michel Gondry is known for creating dream-like worlds. He can do "poetic and lyrical," but his talent also lies in the intense rendering of a simple visual idea. *Fell in Love With a Girl* is an amazingly simple concept, featuring an intricate "Lego-motion" of Jack and Meg White performing. It transforms a performance video into an intricate, painstakingly constructed, and hand-made animated film of primary-colored blocks.

Around the World displays a similar signature visual inventiveness. Daft Punk's techno track is injected with imagery by Gondry, who manages to personify each sound through artistic use of choreography as robot, skeletons, mummies, and synchronized swimmers.

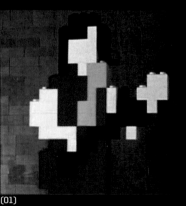

(01)

(02)

(01) *Fell in Love With a Girl*, White Stripes
(02) *Around the World*, Daft Punk

HAMMER & TONGS

■ **IMITATION OF LIFE**
▶ **REM**

■ **COFFEE & TV**
▶ **BLUR**

The director and producer team of Garth Jennings and Nick Goldsmith have an irreverence for the rational. I saw the *Imitation of Life* video while it was being edited at Tongsville HQ in Chinatown, London. It's one of the most amazingly conceptual pieces of video art I have seen. The camera pans and scans, zooming in and out of a short scene of an outdoor, chaotic, all-American party. It is a pop video version of Michelangelo Antonioni's *Blow Up*, examining characters and bringing to life little interactions and absurdities that we never gather from the glance at the big picture.

Coffee & TV, meanwhile, is an affecting tale of an anthropomorphized milk carton adventuring around town in search of a family's lost son (and the song's vocalist, Graham Coxon). It has the taste of the absurd and the familiar, the edgy, and the homely, all in one.

❚❚

[01] *Imitation of Life*, REM

[01]

SPIKE JONZE

(01)

To many, music video didn't grow up until Spike Jonze started making his guerilla sorties into the pop cultural. It is when the form came of age. Ironic, given that the director's work itself has the playfulness of the permanent adolescent. *Sabotage* is his masterpiece. A gonzo homage and parody of 1970s cop shows, the Beastie Boys play the three central characters of Cochese, "The Chief," and Bobby "The Rookie," in the fictional opening credits to the imagined show. The clip illustrates Jonze's talent for the supra-referential, with his videos working atop multiple layers of pop-cultural vernacular.

Weapon of Choice sees a tapdancing Christopher Walken leap into flight around the lobby of the Marriott Hotel in Los Angeles. Its memorable dynamic works on the dislocative association between Walken's famously menacing screen personae, and the affability, whimsy, obvious skill, and expert choreography he shows in this unexpected performance.

FINE CUTS:
HOW TO MAKE
A BETTER VIDEO

For each director featured within this book, you can find a different process, a different way of finding inspiration and creating their music videos. The main thing to realize is that creativity isn't alchemy; there's no magic process. But every director has advice, and develops a personal philosophy on what it takes to make it through the industry.

These are some extracts from their credos to making a better video...

(02)

"I was dancing around wanting to be a filmmaker for a long time but being scared to do it. And creating the RET.Inevitable film festival was part of that—they were these huge-scale cinema installations really. What I learned was that people crave new experiences. People like to be challenged, as long as what you're doing is not pretentious, has some conceptual guts, and is pretty fun."
Adam Levite
(AKA Associates in Science)

(01)

"Music videos still suffer from formula to appeal to mass audiences. Which makes sense from a marketing perspective. But just as music is a visionary soul, so should its visual expression be. More people need to take risks and experiment, even within the mainstream."
+cruz

(03)

"I like to make pretty pictures in Photoshop when pitching on jobs."
Ben Dawkins

(08)

"If I had to say one specific thing that seems to affect people, it's the use of narrative. But that is not any great creative leap on my part. Storytelling and storylistening is something that's ingrained in our DNA. Humans love stories. Beginning, middle, and end is universal. If you can pull it off in a four-minute music video, you are in pretty good shape."
Chris Milk

(04)

"I'm not one to abandon an idea just because there isn't enough money to do it... I'm sure industry people feel that some of my videos aren't slick enough, but I think so long as the ideas and intensions come through, it's all that matters."
Woof Wan-Bau (Joji Koyama)

(06)

"I use the simplest tools and stick to them, and I hardly ever read manuals."
Vernie Yeung

(05)

"Intuition is the thing never to forget, sleep is necessary, and good food always gets everybody doing their best. As a director, it's cool to cook food for the underpaid team. Get the panic out two days before shoot, trust in the fact that you must do this. Live close to your doctor."
Martin de Thurah

(07)

"You need to be fussy with what you work on, as people always know you from the last thing they saw from you. You need to find projects that are ultimately what you want to do. But that's hard, because you can't always pick and choose—you have to make a living."
ne-o

(09)

"When budgets are low, in an effort to shoot something that looks interesting, I often try to find obscure or unusual video cameras or formats."
Adam Levite
(AKA Associates in Science)

▌▌

(01) *Attack of the Ninja*, DJ Uppercut
(02) *NYC*, Interpol
(03) *Man in a Garage*, Coldcut
(04) *Whistle and a Prayer*, Coldcut
(05) *What Else Is There?*, Royksöpp
(06) *I Believe In You*, Kylie

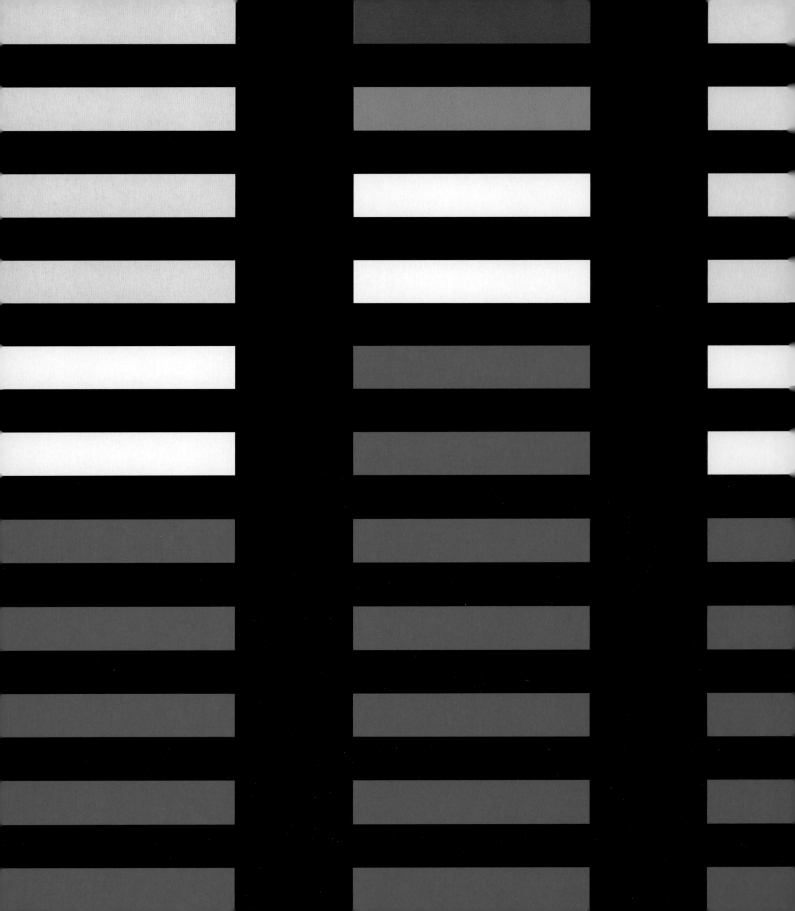

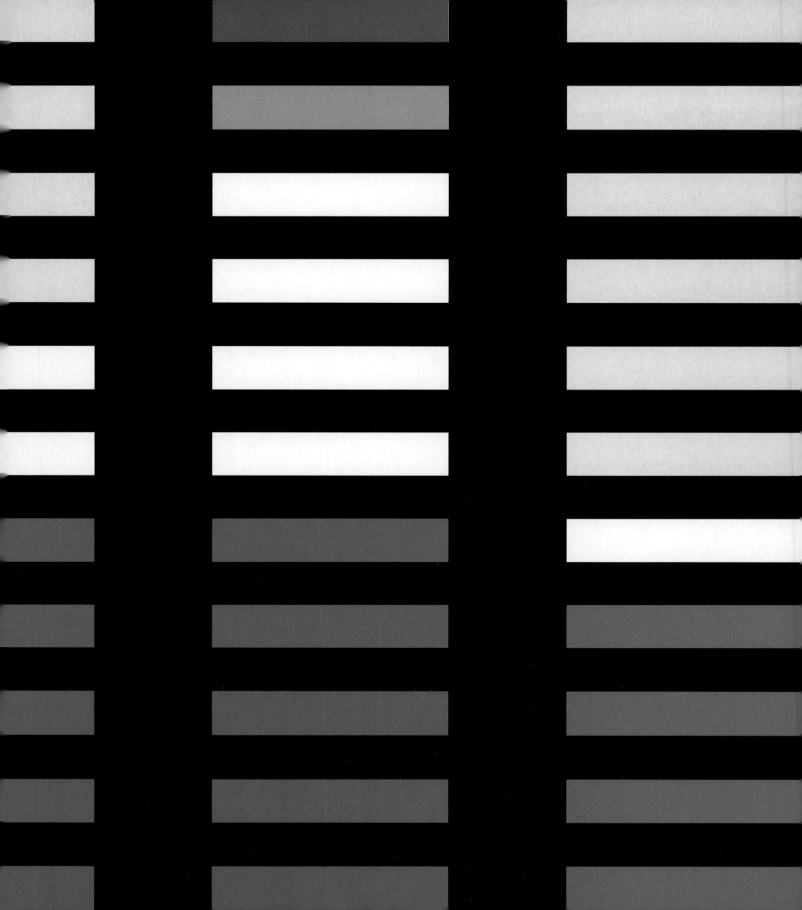

DIGITAL-AGE MUSIC VIDEO: THE DIRECTORS

**ADAM LEVITE
(AKA ASSOCIATES IN SCIENCE)**

BEN DAWKINS

BESSY & COMBE

MARTIN DE THURAH

BRAND NEW SCHOOL

CHRIS MILK

HIDEAKI MOTOKI

PLEIX

RAMON & PEDRO

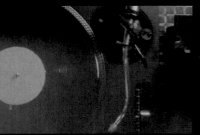

MUTO MASASHI

JONAS ODELL

VERNIE YEUNG

ne-o

+cruz

WOOF WAN-BAU

ADAM LEVITE (AKA ASSOCIATES IN SCIENCE)

VIDEOGRAPHY
IN MY HEAD, QUEENS OF THE STONE AGE
TITO'S WAY, THE JUAN MACLEAN
C'MERE, INTERPOL
ABEL, THE NATIONAL
BLACK TAMBOURINE, BECK
ME AND MIA, TED LEO AND THE PHARMACISTS
SALT THE SKIES, TORTOISE
MISFIT, ELEFANT
A DECADE UNDER THE INFLUENCE, TAKING BACK SUNDAY
MUTESCREAMER, BEANS
ARCTIC SNOW, BURNING BRIDES
MY KIND OF SOLDIER, GUIDED BY VOICES
NYC, INTERPOL (DIRECTED WITH DOUG AITKEN)

"I try to build a framework in which beautiful accidents can happen and then make the video from those moments" ADAM LEVITE

Adam Levite uses everything from super-slo-mo cameras that shoot at 1,000 frames per second, to military-class thermal imaging cameras, in the videos he directs under the moniker AiS/Associates in Science. The naming convention is a stance taken to help him take a step back from the archetypal director's ego, and concentrate on what is going to work for the music artist concerned.

"Directing is something that I have always wanted to do," he elucidates. "And I spent many years dancing around directing: Doing graphic then broadcast design, curating the RET.Inevitable film festival and such. What I do is a pretty natural intersection of all the things that I am interested in and good at: Music, design, art, storytelling, making stuff, and working with people."

Levite's background in graphic design is immediately obvious in his treatment of Beck's *Black Tambourine* video. In one of Levite's most accomplished and high-profile videos to date, the vocalist's

"My previous career as a graphic designer has hugely influenced my work. It taught me to respect my process. I usually work by setting up a framework and then try to let things be very loose and intuitive within that. Honestly, it has allowed me to do interesting videos while still being pretty much an amateur filmmaker. The shots that happen accidentally are often the most exciting. So I try to build a framework in which beautiful accidents can happen and then make the video from those moments.

"The reason I left design was to work with live action—real film, real narrative. I wanted to avoid putting graphic design over pictures—it felt gratuitous and I didn't want to be an animator. I wanted to apply my design process to live action; to make it fractured, iconoclastic, off-kilter—smart, without looking anything like it."

Although many of Levite's contemporaries are critical of the general quality of work that gets broader

So we see a refreshing change in styles across his reel, and a varied approach to performance-based work across, for example, Interpol and The National videos. The plum Beck gig Levite landed last year offered the type of showcasing opportunity directors kill for and a novel approach to moving forward his approach to the artist's performance.

Levite says, "That video was always going to use ASCII. We shot it on digital video first, everyone approved a sequence of shots, and then we applied the effects. When we finally applied the ASCII effect, everyone was like, 'Oh, I miss seeing faces,' which is flattering because everyone liked what we shot so much. But, if I had known that we were going to use it without the effect I would have shot it differently. Without the effect it looks like a Gap ad, and not a very good one. You can see the grasshopper and the Mexican marionette better, though."

Levite's videos feel steeped in the edgy New York milieux in which he

(01)

(02)

(03)

■ BLACK TAMBOURINE
► BECK

Levite worked with his friends at digital artgroup C505 to use an ASCII filter to transform live-action shots of Beck and entourage in the *Black Tambourine* video. Other videos from the album continue to filter these specifically early digital age styles.

"Beck brought the cape and sombrero. The grasshopper was on the wall at our production design meeting so he made it into the video."

Beck begins jabbing at an old typewriter and the characters come to life in a sequence of images made up of ASCII characters.

Levite: "Up until the day before I flew out to LA for the shoot, I had no idea how to make a broadcast-resolution ASCII piece. I knew that, in the worst case, I could make it frame by frame using any of a bunch of ASCII apps or Web sites." >>>

■

(01–13) Final filtered ASCII video footage and raw performance video
[02, 04, 07, 09] Raw video footage showing comparisons to final filtered shots

(04)

(05)

(06)

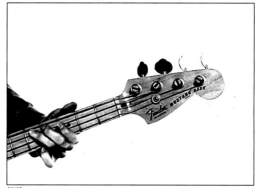

(07)

(08)

(09)

(10)

(11)

(12)

(13)

● SLATE

STYLE: **PERFORMANCE, ANIMATION**
DISTINGUISHING FEATURE:
CUSTOM ASCII SOFTWARE BY C505
PROCESS: **DV CAMERA**
VIDEO FOR ALBUM: *GUERO*, BECK

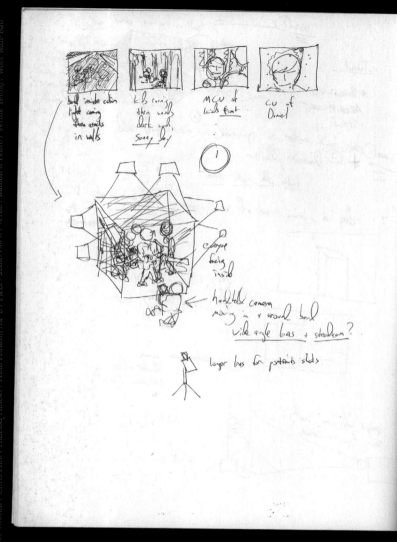

Adam Levite AKA Associates in Science / Bessy & Combe / Brand New School / Ben Dawkins / Martin de Thurah / Chris Milk / Hideaki Motoki / Muto Musashi /mc o / Flexx / Jonas Odell / +cruz / Ramon & Pedro / Verne Yeung / Woof Wan-Bau

◼ C'MERE
▶ INTERPOL

Playing like a contemporary fable, a beautiful witch and children track the band to a wooden Hansel and Gretel-style shack in a snow-laden forest. They promptly begin to set this alight; the visual twist being the flames and gowns that adorn them are made from flowing, undulating, fabric.

Levite says, "I love this video because it's so weird. We shot all the outdoor stuff during a single, short winter's day, using all natural light, and after fighting traffic from New York City out to the country. The fabrics on the kids and witch were all custom-made for the shoot."

▋▋

(01) Original sketches, showing camera and lighting angles and production notes
(02–09) Video stills

● SLATE

STYLE: **OUTDOOR NARRATIVE, PERFORMANCE**
DISTINGUISHING FEATURE: **CUSTOM-BUILT WOODEN SHACK, CUSTOM FABRIC COSTUMES**
PROCESS: **16MM FILM WITH FLAME DIGITAL POST EFFECTS (THE MILL, NY)**
VIDEO FOR THE ALBUM: *ANTICS*, INTERPOL

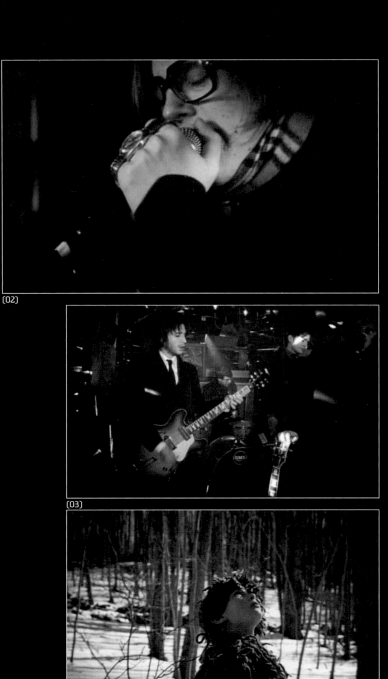

(02)

(03)

(04)

(05)

(06)

(07)

(08)

(09)

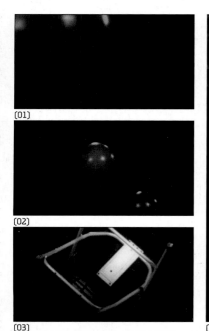

(01)

(02)

(03)

(04)

■ SALT THE SKIES
▶ TORTOISE

Levite considers this his best concept in one sentence: "We will throw things at the band and shoot them jumping out of the way at 1,000 frames per second."

The video is filmed in a highly minimalistic fashion, locked-off shots documenting everything from chairs, colored balls, pencils, plush dolls, and household plants floating in space against a black backdrop. And generally toward, and presumably hitting, band members.

"I am pretty hard on myself, so I don't think many of my videos are that successful, but if my arm were twisted I would say that the *Tortoise* and *Taking Back Sunday* concepts were pretty successful. I feel like there is a good match between the video, the mood of the song, and the vibe of the band." >>>

(05)

(06)

● SLATE

STYLE: INDOOR, ABSTRACT FILM
DISTINGUISHING FEATURE:
SLOW MOTION
PROCESS: IN CAMERA
VIDEO FOR THE ALBUM: *IT'S ALL
AROUND YOU*, TORTOISE

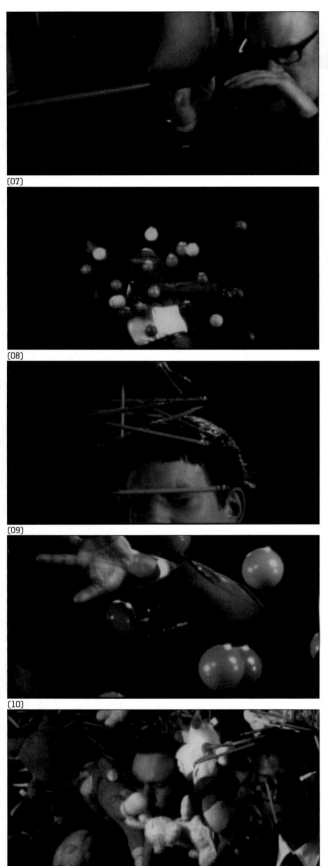

(07)

(08)

(09)

(10)

(11)

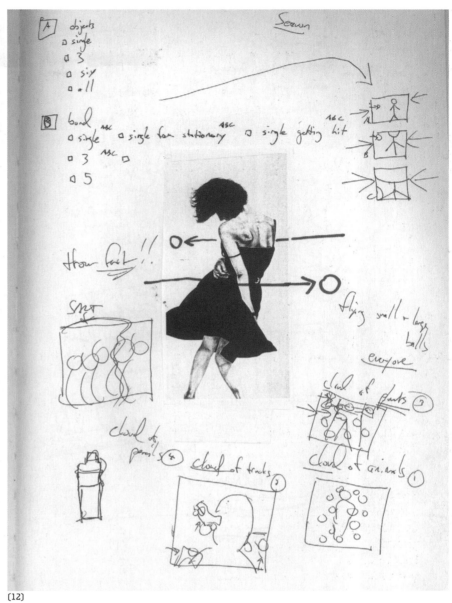

(12)

II (01–11) Live-action performance, shot at 1,000 frames per second
(12) Production notes detailing movement and camera angles

(01)

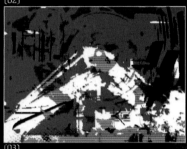
(02)

(03)

(04)

(05)

(06)

● SLATE

STYLE: **TREATED CAMERAWORK**
MAIN EFFECT: **THERMAL IMAGING, NIGHTVISION**
PROCESS: **THERMAL IMAGING CAMERA, NIGHTVISION CAMERA**
VIDEO FOR THE ALBUM: *TURN ON THE BRIGHT LIGHTS*, INTERPOL

■ NYC
► INTERPOL

"The label and band were freaked out because the song was called *NYC* and we shot among all these abandoned airplane wrecks," says Adam Levite. "They didn't want people to think the song or the video were about 9/11—which they obviously weren't. So, at the time, I think they were worried about what we did. Paul Banks (of Interpol) later told me that it's one of his favorite videos."

■■
(01–08) *NYC*, Interpol. Video stills using nightvision, thermal imaging, and graphic elements

Adam Levite AKA Associates in Science

⏸ [01–04]

TITO'S WAY
THE JUAN MACLEAN

A simple idea of using crude stop motion to segue between instructional combat images, using subtle still graphic overlays for impacts and captioning. "I used an old US army self-defense manual as our shot list," says Levite.

[05–06]

ABEL
THE NATIONAL

"We shot in the band's practice space and their house in Brooklyn," explains Levite. "You can feel their comfort and naturalness in their surroundings." Levite's graphic affinities come through in subtle, simple shots, the autumnal colors and faded hues of this intimate performance video.

[07]

A DECADE UNDER THE INFLUENCE
TAKING BACK SUNDAY

One of Levite's favorites, it communicates a raw energy. A searing flashlight against a darkened stage distorts the band while the camera revolves. Levite: "We shot it next to an indoor skate ramp in Brooklyn—the guys who built the ramp built the set. The cameras and spots circled the band on radio-controlled cars."

[08]

MISFIT
ELEFANT

"A homage to Duran Duran's *Girls on Film*," explains Levite.

[09]

PULK/PULL REVOLVING DOORS
RADIOHEAD SPEC VIDEO

Reflects an anxiety and jitterishness perfect for the track, with fluttering images literally shaking the cityscape from its foundations. The layered images, bleached-out city detail, and speeded-up construction illustrate the process of things. A reflection of Levite's transition from graphics to film. ■

[01]

[02]

[03]

[04]

[05]

[06]

[07]

[08]

[09]

BESSY & COMBE

VIDEOGRAPHY

PEACE RUNNING, PANASONIC SHORT FILM
DEUX PIEDS, THOMAS FERSEN
YALIL, MICKEY 3D
RESPIRE, MICKEY 3D (WITH STÉPHANE HAMACHE)

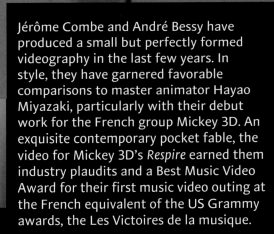

Jérôme Combe and André Bessy have produced a small but perfectly formed videography in the last few years. In style, they have garnered favorable comparisons to master animator Hayao Miyazaki, particularly with their debut work for the French group Mickey 3D. An exquisite contemporary pocket fable, the video for Mickey 3D's *Respire* earned them industry plaudits and a Best Music Video Award for their first music video outing at the French equivalent of the US Grammy awards, the Les Victoires de la musique.

Bessy & Combe make micro adventures of epic proportions and intimate contortions, as can be seen in their fluid animations; music videos for Thomas Fersen, Mickey 3D, and short films including *Peace Running* for Panasonic's Capture the Motion series.

The creative team met by chance through living in the same area of Paris, and combined their diverse backgrounds—Jérôme honed his 3D skills through creating videogame visuals, while André started out in screenwriting—to tackle more complex adult narrative and realistic settings within the context of computer-generated and, in particular, 3D imagery.

"The 3D world has been the small, protected world of a handful of specialists for a long time, and we thought it interesting to open it up to a wider audience who would identify better with classic storylines and emotions, but surprise them with a unique style," they explain.

Since 2002 and their test for an animated feature film, *Bizarre Love Triangle*, they have used music as a way to hang these contemporary fables. They are video directors who care less about sonic visuals then they do about weaving obvious narrative ambition around sound, using this to drive the mood of a story.

"We often find that trends and movements don't take into account the specificities of each individual. The only true direction we follow is the one our characters follow" BESSY & COMBE

"Our esthetic is a hybrid between traditional animated cartoons, adult comics and arthouse cinema," they say, eschewing the notion that their animation is quintessential of the new French look in the area.

"I guess thinking that we are 'French' in our style is a bit too narrow a description for us," they insist. "Even though our cultural references are quite obvious, we often look toward Asia, the UK, and the independent part of the US, often in complete clash with its traditional culture."

Bessy & Combe skim around the culture of music video, so the technical and stylistic drive inherent in much of the next-generation work is backgrounded —a direct contrast to the work of many of their contemporaries in the field who deliberately explore this side. Instead what is most evocative is the characterization, whether it be the Parisian slacker esthetic of Thomas Fersen, Le Parkour "street gymnastics" of the protagonist in *Peace Running*, or the central character of the little girl in *Respire* and the follow-up, *Yalil*.

An urban equivalent of Chihiro, the 10-year-old girl in Miyazaki's *Spirited Away*, *Respire*'s heroine cavorts in a virtual realized countryside, before sinister glitches, artificial forms, and CCTV cameras intrude and bring her back to a drab world of gray, manmade forms and unfeeling crowds.

"We often find that music videos lack originality and depth," they explain. "In the 1980s and up to the mid 1990s, it was a great experimental field for innovative directors such as Anton Corbijn, Derek Jarman, Jean-Baptiste Mondino or, closer to us, Chris Cunningham, Spike Jonze, and Michel Gondry."

They complain about the passivity of the performance video, and have sidestepped this by using motion capture in the *Deux Pieds* music video to capture Thomas Fersen as one of the actors in the scenario. One of the hallmarks of their work is to push super-realistic depiction of character movement alongside a gritty urban story.

Their process: "First and foremost, we discuss the idea; whether we create it from scratch or we get a detailed brief. The story is always our starting point, whatever the circumstances of the project. Then we go on to writing a more technical memo with the initial transitions and framings. It then moves into an animatic to tailor the direction for each shot. When we are fully happy with this 'shot storyboard,' we can move on to the production itself.

"We like working with smallish teams to stay in control. We are obsessed with the fluidity of the movements in our characters, so they appear as natural and realistic as possible. We often use motion capture but always have a good animator correcting the stiffness of the moves it sometimes gives. We also do all the editing ourselves, as, for us, this is where the true directing comes into play."

For all the childlike innocence on the surface of the diptych of Mickey 3D videos—with allusions to *The Truman Show* and *Soylent Green*—it actually becomes an indictment of both reality shows and over-urbanism, deliberately "militant."

Deux Pieds' doomed romanticism—with a lover late for a rendezvous left to play videogames at a fastfood joint while his paramour absconds with BMW-man—signals their more hard-edged influences. They mention the frank photography of Juergen Teller, the hard-boiled graphic novels of Frank Miller, alongside the lyrical verité of Jean-Luc Godard, and of Wong Kar-Wai. Significantly, their most recent short film work, *Peace Running*, presents a more maxed-out, stark, and kinetic run through a monochrome city. Once again, the hero is trying to outrun, being captured within its hellish confines through Le Parkour leaps over wire fences and rolls off trucks.

When these influences come together with their most intriguing influence—the supercharged sensuality of Milo Manara, the Italian erotic comic book artist (you can see it hard at work in that first test film, *Bizarre Love Triangle*)—they might well create the adult masterpiece they are obviously striving for. Surely it would be an opportunity too good to resist for the right female vocalist? Commissioners should take note. >>>

(01)

"We wanted to plunge our two characters into different times, completely paradoxically," say the duo. "The hero belonged to the world of the slow and his fiancée to that of speed. The goal was to show that their relationship could not function because one evolves and moves against the rhythm of the other. Thanks to motion capture, we could render two opposed gestures: One untied, flexible, nonchalant; and the other rather nervous, abrupt with a direction—sometimes with rather slow camera movements, sometimes with sharp movements, handheld on the shoulder— adapting to the speed of the two characters.

"We also wanted to make Paris a character in this story, with a complete part to play in it. We made the story setting very urban, so you felt the action could take place only in such a city."

Thomas Fersen played himself in the shoot, which simultaneously captured several actors. If revered Italian director Michelangelo Antonioni ever made a cel-shaded 3D music video, it might look something like this. Highly naturalistic animated performances are captured as a couple awaken in a typically déshabillé Parisian apartment, and a daydreaming boyfriend is left twiddling his thumbs around their re-imagined Atari Atra-I arcade machine, rather than a sweet caress from his would-be girlfriend. >>>

(02)

(03)

(04)

(05)

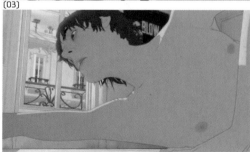

(06)

(07)

(08)

II

(01–08) Fluid motion-captured animation
in *Deux Pieds* for Thomas Fersen
(09–10) Animation test key frames

Adam Levite AKA Associates in Science / Ben Dawkins / Brand New School / Bessy & Combe / Martin de Thurah / Chris Milk / Hideaki Motoki / Muto Musashi /ne-o / Pleix / Jonas Odell / +cruz / Ramon & Pedro / Vernie Yeung / Woof Wan-Bau

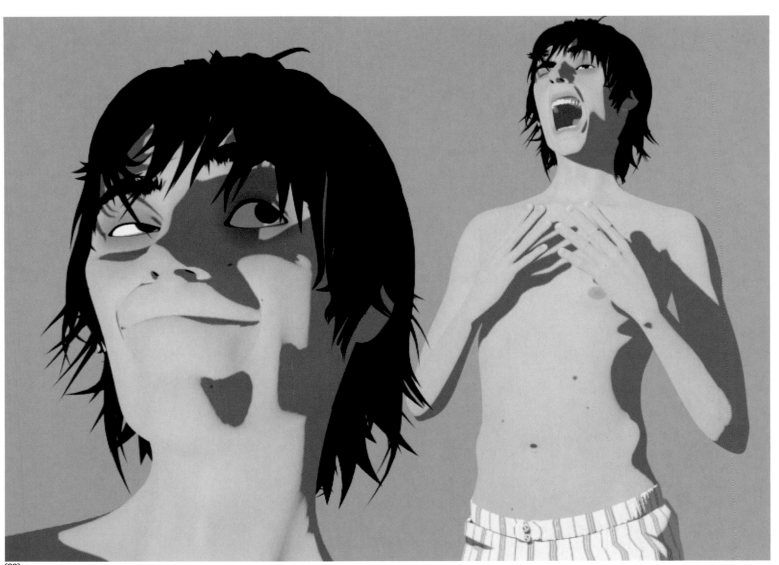

(09)

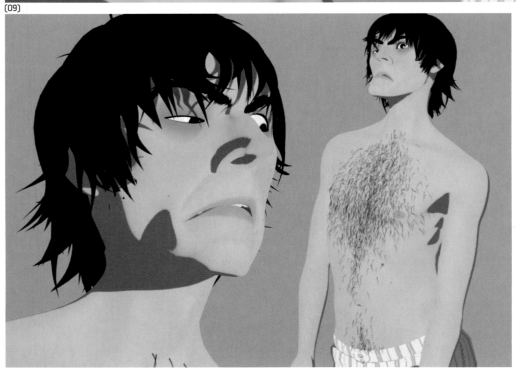

(10)

● SLATE

STYLE: ANIMATED ADVENTURE
DISTINGUISHING FEATURE:
MUTED PASTELS AND MOTION
CAPTURED ANIMATION
PROCESS: MOTION CAPTURED
ANIMATION WITH 3D STUDIO MAX
VIDEO FOR ALBUM: *PIÈCE MONTÉE
DES GRANDS JOURS*, THOMAS FERSEN

(01)

(02)

(03)

■ YALIL / RESPIRE
► MICKEY 3D
WITH STÉPHANE HAMACHE

A virtual reality playground is a refuge for kids in an dystopic, overcrowded near-future/present. A young girl frolicks through artificially generated hills and Disney-esque woodland before the azure blue sky snaps to static and we are back in a world of CCTV and drab city streets.

"It was great to be able to work on two consecutive music videos for the same group," say Bessy & Combe. "It allowed us to establish the character of the little girl—probably an orphan and maybe homeless—looking for warmth. She's the David Copperfield of a near-apocalyptic future. Despite the chaotic environment she evolves in, she represents the energy of life. So in both videos, lots of very positive thinking!" >>>

● SLATE

STYLE: ANIMATED ADVENTURE
DISTINGUISHING FEATURE: DECEPTIVELY SIMPLE YET INTRICATE ANIMATION
PROCESS: 3D STUDIO MAX, CARTOON REYES AND COMBUSTION
VIDEO FOR ALBUM: *TU VAS PAS MOURIR DE RIRE*, MICKEY 3D

(01) *Respire*, Mickey 3D
(02–09) *Yalil*, Mickey 3D
(10) Storyboard for *Respire*, Mickey 3D

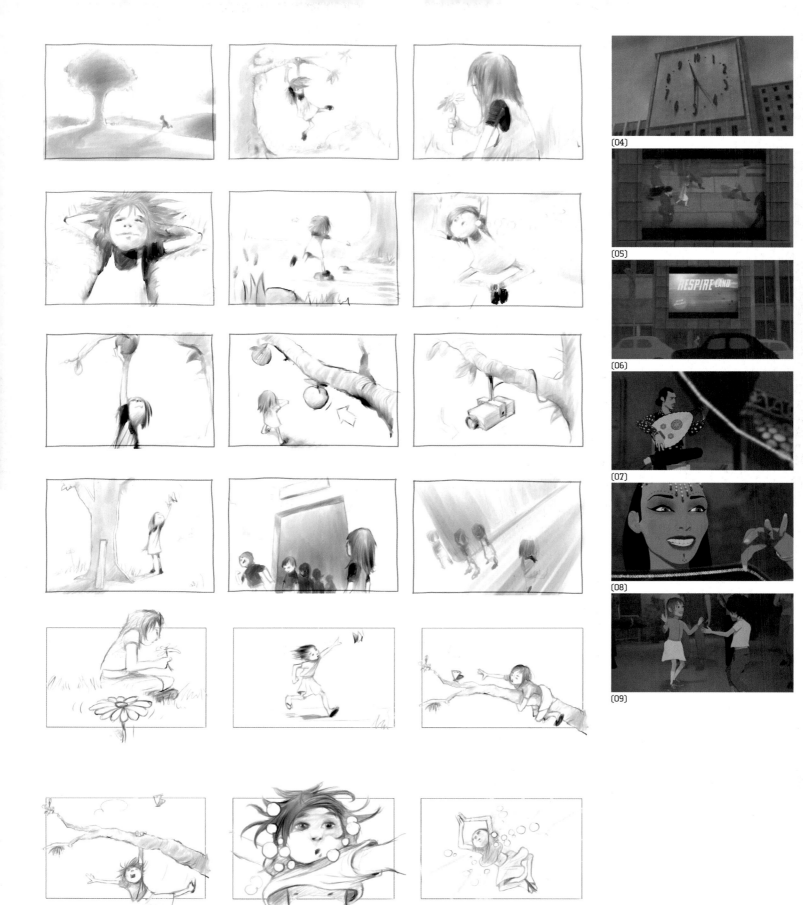

(04)

(05)

(06)

(07)

(08)

(09)

(10)

PEACE RUNNING
PANASONIC
SHORT FILM

"We opted for a black and white render, which makes it possible to create a heavy, oppressive atmosphere," say Bessy & Combe "The only note of hope that asserts itself in the darkness is the red witness. The montage, which is dynamic and choppy, should present a notion of urgency, speed and emphasis, using the widest possible angles, the epic effort of the runner. The sound also comes in to equally reinforce the required effect—it is a mixture of muffled and saturated noises underlining the imminent danger that threatens the city. Thus creating suspense, as in a thriller film."

Part of a series of short films tied to Panasonic's involvement in the last Summer Olympic games, *Peace Running* for Capture the Motion was the stand-out short of the series. Featuring fluid black-and-white vectors, heavily refined through After Effects and Final Cut Pro work, a runner dashes to escape a folding page/ shadow falling over a chiaroscuroed cityscape with his red furled document/baton.

[01]

[02]

[03]

■ BIZARRE LOVE TRIANGLE
► FILM TEST

(01)

(02)

(03)

(04)

(05)

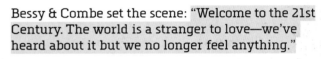

(06)

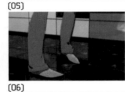

(07)

(08)

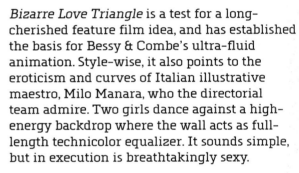

(09)

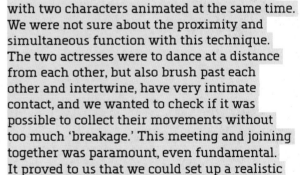

(10)

(11)

Bessy & Combe set the scene: "Welcome to the 21st Century. The world is a stranger to love—we've heard about it but we no longer feel anything."

Bizarre Love Triangle is a test for a long-cherished feature film idea, and has established the basis for Bessy & Combe's ultra-fluid animation. Style-wise, it also points to the eroticism and curves of Italian illustrative maestro, Milo Manara, who the directorial team admire. Two girls dance against a high-energy backdrop where the wall acts as full-length technicolor equalizer. It sounds simple, but in execution is breathtakingly sexy.

"It is, in fact, our first test of motion capture with two characters animated at the same time. We were not sure about the proximity and simultaneous function with this technique. The two actresses were to dance at a distance from each other, but also brush past each other and intertwine, have very intimate contact, and we wanted to check if it was possible to collect their movements without too much 'breakage.' This meeting and joining together was paramount, even fundamental. It proved to us that we could set up a realistic and adult universe in the 3D field."

II

(01–11) Motion capture of two dancers simultaneously animated

BRAND NEW SCHOOL

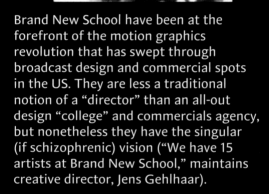

VIDEOGRAPHY

HYSTERIA, MUSE
LIGHT AND DAY, POLYPHONIC SPREE
STAND, JEWEL (CO-DIRECTED WITH CHRIS APPLEBAUM)
HANDS DOWN, DASHBOARD CONFESSIONAL (DIRECTED BY NZINGHA STEWART)

Brand New School have been at the forefront of the motion graphics revolution that has swept through broadcast design and commercial spots in the US. They are less a traditional notion of a "director" than an all-out design "college" and commercials agency, but nonetheless they have the singular (if schizophrenic) vision ("We have 15 artists at Brand New School," maintains creative director, Jens Gehlhaar).

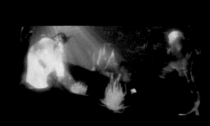

Brand New School have a great reputation built mainly on their commercials work. But, surprisingly, if you take out their co-direction credits, they are only responsible for just two music videos. They have learnt from previous collaborations with outside directors the hard way, and are adamant that only solely directed work will be seen from them in the future ("That's kind of a dead road to go down now," notes BNS founder, Jonathan Notaro).

With only a handful of previous music video clips—for Polyphonic Spree and Muse—but a huge amount of commercial spots, their work is the epitome of the finely crafted, supremely executed motion graphics treatment that US creatives do so well. But like any good directors, they are fighting against being pigeonholed.

"For too many people, this industry is about styles," argues Notaro. "If anything, we create a style and then abandon it. I am more concerned about not being a one-trick pony, and having a greater breadth to our work while retaining a voice, not a style. Just by nature of being a visual person, I am attracted to not looking one way. We use lots of different vernaculars. Our biggest concern is to keep moving forward."

Gehlhaar adds: "The question is really about when an individual gets bored repeating themselves. We want to grow; not in numbers, but with the quality, size, and exposure of the jobs we do, and that means saying no to stuff."

Notaro adds, "Our goal is to have only a few really good projects going on in each office, and then do a video every four to six months. We want to wait for the right songs to come along."

"We use lots of different vernaculars. Our biggest concern is to keep moving forward" JONATHAN NOTARO

It's a fine position to maneuver oneself into, and BNS have striven to become a bicoastal shop that can cater to the right bespoke project. Gehlhaar explains: "It's a weird ride in this industry. This thing 'motion graphics'—a term that we started hating and stopped using—is going bad. There is a lot of hack work happening, and there are so many new companies doing what we and a few others started."

Notaro and Gehlhaar, who act as principal directors of the company's videos, are acutely aware of steering the right path for themselves in a market that eats up the new, chews it for creativity, then spits it out, ready for the next crop of talent.

"It's very odd and interesting right now, but it's clear to me that just mastering the techniques of hybrid animation and live action is not the path to glory," Gehlhaar elucidates. "You have to develop your own voice, and not bank on the idea that this whole thing will still be cool three years from now. Remember that a whole bunch of directors with film backgrounds can get their CG done at The Mill, too."

These are wise words of caution for anyone entering the industry. BNS don't suffer from any delusions about the commercial pressures of the music video industry—its restrictions or its opportunities. Despite this, they come across as optimistic and excited by the form and its future.

"Music videomaking, for us, is a forum to try out new ideas or techniques," confesses Notaro. "There's less of a budget, less pressure, and less of a media buy, so it won't be as big a failure if it doesn't work out! A lot of commercial ideas come out of videos we've done. I suppose this is the reason why a lot of directors use music videos to sharpen their skills. It's kind of a shorthand evolution of a director: Make crappy films in film school, move on through music videos, up to commercials, and then maybe get to shoot a feature. I don't agree with this hierarchy, but that's how many people see it.

"It's funny, because we have done way more commercials than music videos, so we don't really need to step up and prove ourselves in commercials any more. I actually want to do more music videos, especially now, where there are new outlets for them."

Gehlhaar, in particular, is fired up by the current possibilities in the form created by the new online and distribution methods, and the opportunities it presents to the director as an "author" of the work rather than simply a "hired hand."

"I think, in general, there are three kinds of music videos," he states. "The archetypal formulas for EMO, hip-hop, anger rock, whatever the genre, are mostly performances intercut with other sets or little stories. Within each genre, they all look the same. Then there's the music video that gets shown at Resfest or onedotzero, where the song is not necessarily the strong part, but the visuals are amazing. The third kind is where the sound and visuals are of equal strength—like those great Spike Jonze or Jonathan Glazer videos. Those guys usually just work for really great songs, and add to them."

What's interesting is how their two defining videos—outside the work created for Jewel, Dashboard Confessional, and others, that involved working in tandem with other directorial talent—offer the twin perspectives of working with music artists. >>>

[01]

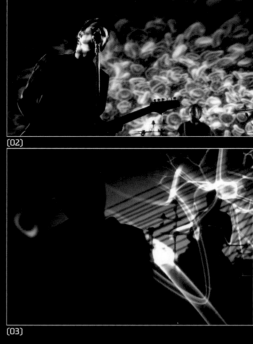

[02]

[03]

Gehlhaar: "Muse's A&R person, Perry Watts-Russell, had worked with Radiohead before and mentioned how different the attitudes between bands regarding their visual image was. With Radiohead, at least lead singer Thom Yorke was highly interested in the process of creating images for music, and very involved with the making of the video, whereas Matthew Bellamy from Muse didn't seem to care much. He focusses completely on the music. It's a matter of temperament. If a musician is very involved in conceiving a video, it might lead to a great, unpredictable, non-formulaic piece. Or, when the musicians don't let the director do what they do best, it might lead to a video full of cliches."

Notaro offers the opposite experience: "Tim DeLaughter from Polyphonic Spree is a very visual person, and he was very involved in the shoot. He was in the band The Tripping Daisies before, and what he learnt from that experience is that he wanted to manage his own image better with this new project. He had so many references. His frame of reference might have been very one-sided, but it was commendable that he brought some things to the table. He really liked the old Disney-style of animation. So he brought something in regard to how he wanted the tone of the video to be rather than the actual look."

Brand New School's process is very much about being in control of their destiny as much as a creative method. They've painstakingly and commendably built a production infrastructure on the two coasts of the US to allow them more control of their destiny. With this infrastructure and the possibilities it offers, it is Gehlhaar who succinctly explains why they are still drawn to the form: "Our agenda is to produce self-contained art. We have suffered quite a bit from explaining to people what it is we are doing when we do ads or network stuff. With a music video, people instinctively understand how you conceived and made it. If you are named the director, you wrote it. With a commercial, it is a bit more muddy. You direct somebody else's script. That can be great, if it's a great script, but what is occasionally boring with advertising is that it's always so damn positive. That's another argument for doing music videos: It allows us to explore our darker sides. That's why I loved Muse's *Hysteria*, we could use imagery we could never in a million years use in ads."

■■

[01–03] Muse perform against an invasive backdrop of medical and abstract imagery
[04–05] Storyboard development integrates live band performance with temporary graphic elements
[06] Graphic elements offering inspiration in the pre-production process

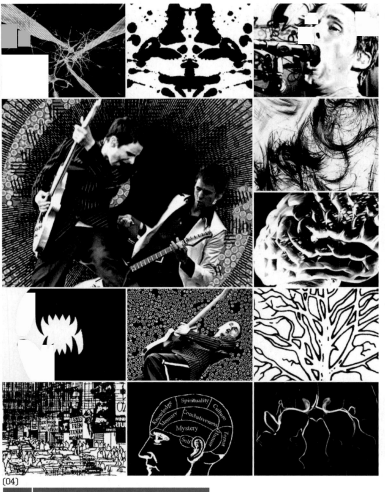

[04]

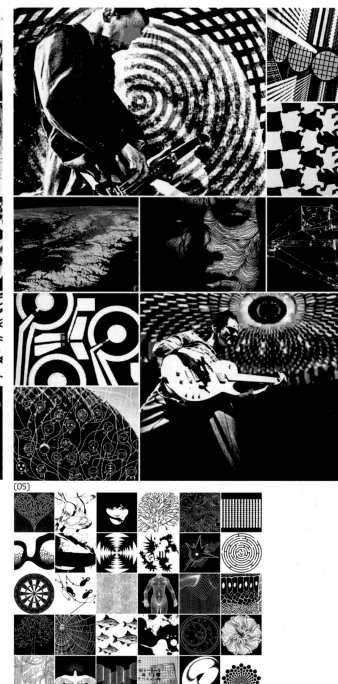

[05]

■ HYSTERIA
▶ MUSE

Hysteria is a dark performance video with a twist. Capturing an intense set by Muse, a video backdrop conveys medical imagery related to the nerves twined, and the blood coursing through the human body. As the track grows, the imagery explodes into 3D, flowing through the space and the band's performance.

Gehlhaar: "When I write video treatments for a band that already looks cool and performs great, I just want to put them into a great space and let them do their thing. We got lucky with Muse as they are so incredibly good as a live band, although we weren't familiar with them when we wrote the treatment." >>>

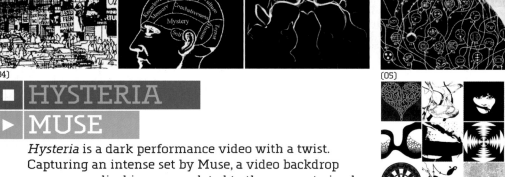

[06]

● SLATE

STYLE: PERFORMANCE WITH MOTION GRAPHICS
DISTINGUISHING FEATURE: SUBTLE INTEGRATION OF GRAPHIC EFFECTS INTO PREDOMINANT LIVE ACTION
PROCESS: FILM CAMERA WITH MOTION GRAPHIC COMPOSITING
VIDEO FOR ALBUM: *ABSOLUTION*, MUSE

> 00:00 BASS RIFF

SHOT 001 SHOT 002 SHOT 003 SHOT 004

> 00:10 BASS RIFF + DRUMS

SHOT 005 SHOT 006 SHOT 007

Raw dots cut on and off, white dots pile up over black dots

Dots get cut up in sync with the drums; snare drum hits turns curves into angular shapes

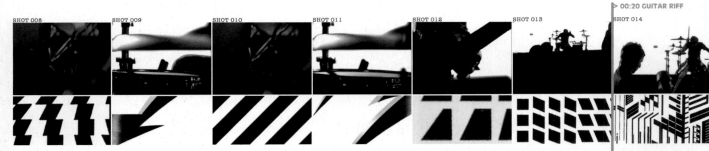

SHOT 008 SHOT 009 SHOT 010 SHOT 011 SHOT 012 SHOT 013

> 00:20 GUITAR RIFF

SHOT 014

Angular shapes make more complex pattern; animations hold over two beats or so

(01)

(02)

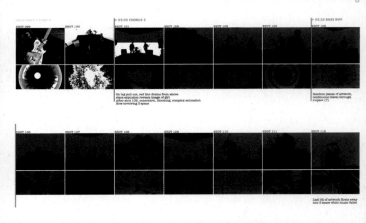

(03)

Adam Levite AKA Associates in Science / Bessy & Combs / Brand New School / Ben Dawkins / Martin de Thurah / Chris Milk / Hideaki Motoki / Motomichi Nakamura / Flexx / Jonas Odell / Cruz / Ramon & Pedro / Vernie Yeung / Woof Wan-Bau

II

(01–03) The band's green-screen performance
storyboarded against the video backdrop

[04]

[05]

[06]

[07]

[08]

[09]

[10]

[11]

[12]

[04–12] Brand New School twist the rock band performance video with color bleed and a backdrop that comes alive

(01)

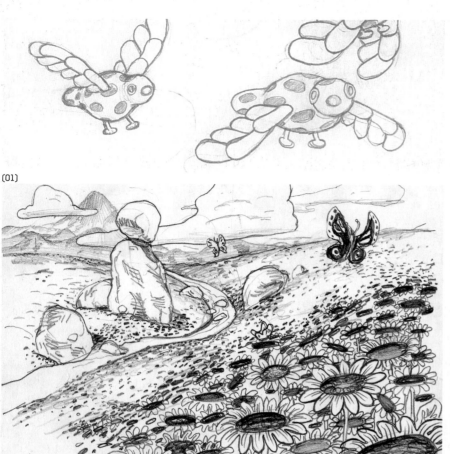

(02)

(03)

(04)

(05)

LIGHT AND DAY
▶ POLYPHONIC SPREE

A technicolor, hyperreal, Disney-esque fantasy
sees the begowned band members follow the sun...
While some elements might be too literal, the
animated execution and production design offer
an exuberant vision that is a perfect complement
to Polyphonic Spree's feelgood anthem.

Notaro: "You could argue that *Light and Day* is
really a glorified performance video. The band is
amazing to look at, after all—24 people in white robes!
But because I am not a musician, I usually think
there needs to be something else in a video—lots
of directors feel that way. Here, there was another
idea going on: The quest for the light. It was nice to
just show the band and embellish it with graphics.
I had my hesitations about that simplicity, but
halfway through the shoot, after all sorts of things
went wrong, I thought 'We just need to shoot them
performing, and it's going to be alright.'" >>>

● SLATE

STYLE: MOTION GRAPHICS PERFORMANCE
DISTINGUISHING FEATURE: GROUP MEMBERS
POPULATE ENVISIONED FANTASY LAND
PROCESS: FILM CAMERA WITH ANIMATION
AND HEAVY POSTPRODUCTION COMPOSITING
VIDEO FOR ALBUM: *THE BEGINNING
STAGES OF...*, THE POLYPHONIC SPREE

[06]  [07]  [08]  [09]  [10]  [11]  [12]  [13] 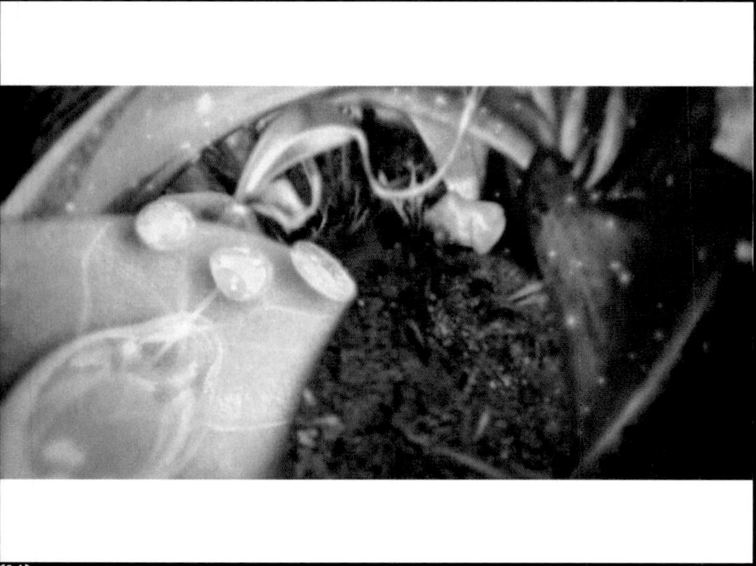 [14]  [15]  [16]

II

[01–02] Concept illustrations
[03-16] The 24-strong band composited against and within a fairytale graphic world

BEN DAWKINS

VIDEOGRAPHY

MAN IN A GARAGE,	COLDCUT
IS THIS A REAL CITY,	JIMMY EDGAR
BREATHLESS,	NICK CAVE & THE BAD SEEDS
LITTLE THOUGHTS,	BLOC PARTY
RPMDAP TRACK 6,	BOGDAN RACZYNSKI

Character design isn't something only the Japanese are good at. Ben Dawkins proves that there is more to British animated characters than *Wallace & Gromit*. The English director has quickly amassed an unreal menagerie of virtual characters: Sprites, cute apes, and other strange imaginary friends and animals.

His first, a square-headed, diminutive red pixel-sprite, was his directorial calling card. The star of a Bogdan Raczynski promo for cult electronic label, Rephlex Records, the 1 foot (30cm) high figure breakdances around a friend's lounge to get noticed. When sent to production companies, the video received a stony silence, but its star, Little Bogdan, soon got the attention he deserved online.

"I sent the finished result to lots of production companies on DVD and didn't get much response, so I uploaded it to a simple Web page," explains Dawkins. "After about two months, I'd had over 500,000 hits. I'd been to New York to pitch on a massive job for Spike TV. And then Mother ad agency awarded me three Orange commercials. Bogdan went on to receive tons of press, which launched my full-time directing career.

"Bogdan was the result of three months' hard work, completed while I was working as a full-time motion graphic designer. Evenings, weekends, lunch breaks—any free time—was quickly consumed. I've always wanted to get into music video direction. I made Bogdan to get into the industry, but have had much more success as a commercials director, which is lucky, I guess."

On graduating from Bournemouth & Poole College of Art and Design in 1997, Dawkins put his digital photography and illustration knowledge to work as a photographer's assistant. Via a stint in print graphics, he made the transition to direction through 3D and computer-generated animation work. Through Bogdan and a short film/promo completed for the Warp vs *Creative Review* 2005 competition for Warp artist Jimmy Edgar, Dawkins has built a particular reputation for innovative integration of live action with both abstract and "realistic" visual effects work. The latter work helped secure him a Best Director nomination at the UK Music Vision awards (formerly the CADS) in 2005.

"*Who Framed Roger Rabbit?* did something to me. It used to be a challenge for the people at Disney to integrate live action and animation, but these days, with the technology available, it's just a case of learning the process" BEN DAWKINS

"Lets face it. You do something everyone likes and you are pigeonholed forever," says Dawkins. Yet he concedes the area he's recognized for is wide open for interpretation, so it's not all bad. And he has quickly built a successful niche for himself that is allowing him to branch out, while receiving a steady stream of both commercial and promo opportunities.

The pros: "Designing characters is fun. Doing on-set special effects is even more so. It requires a lot of planning, which is how I like to work. All the massive commercial directors do it as well, which is a nice feeling." And the cons? "It can be incredibly time consuming once it has been shot," he says, referring to the heavy visual effects work necessary for integrating characters into the footage. "If the budget is low, I have to do it all myself, which does nothing for my mental health."

Combining artificial characters and elements in live space carries its own particular challenges. Dawkins explains: "What can I say? *Who Framed Roger Rabbit?* did something to me. It used to be a challenge for the people at Disney to integrate live action and animation, but these days, with the technology available, it's just a case of learning the process. I completed Bogdan on my trusty G4 Powerbook, in my bedroom. Once you know the process, it's all up to your imagination."

Luckily for his sanity, Dawkins had help creating a flying robotic stork for Sony

Dawkins' work stands out from his UK directorial contemporaries because, alongside his technical precision, he shows promise of exploring more. His music videos are less about generating a distinct visual style than they are about creating an atmosphere—an instant hermetic world—that extends into narrative, location, and social setting. A sketcher of space, Dawkins twists nature and the unnatural into an intimate embrace.

While Bogdan and Bloc Party reference an 8-bit video game esthetic of *Jet Set Willy* (an old ZX Spectrum game), and *Tetris* (the Gameboy blockbuster), new work sees him shifting toward a more cinematic frame of reference. *Man In A Garage*, from the Coldcut album *Sound Mirrors*, plays with a subtle nighttime apparition scenario. It may seem strange, but this new context for his work fits seamlessly with the past.

Citing *Ringu*, Hideo Nakata's cult movie (1998), it's clear that Dawkins is influenced by Japanese horror cinema. I would say that the yokai—arrogant Japanese spirits, demons, and apparitions that are staple figures populating the genre—are the grown-up equivalents and the malevolent relatives to the impish creations Dawkins has previously generated. It will be fascinating to see whether he continues to tread further into the darkness. >>>

A spooky capsule narrative set at twilight has Dawkins focussing on atmosphere and camerawork above obvious effects work.

"The initial brief was set out by the band," says Dawkins. "A man on his way to work stops in a garage and gets a random phone call from a girl in trouble. What does he do?

"I pushed the idea a little further, giving it a ghostly feel. I love horror movies—especially *Ringu* and *Blair Witch*—so that's where the girl and creepy woodland environment come from. We filmed from 12pm–12am (as the budget was tiny) and managed to get 70 per cent of the shots I wanted.

"Very little post was needed for the finished result. Framestore did an amazing grade and some beautiful lighting effects." >>>

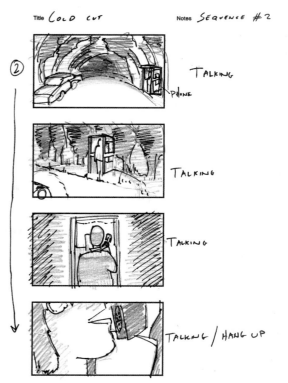

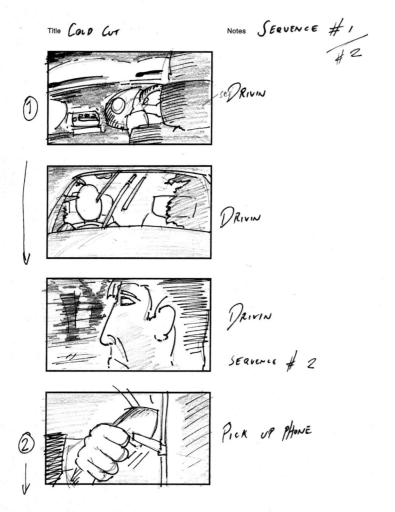

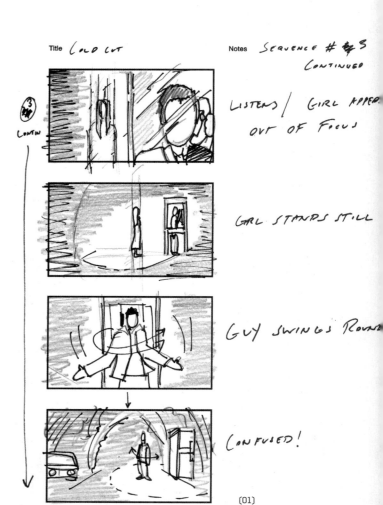

Adam Levite AKA Associates in Science / Bessy & Combe / Brand New School   Ben Dawkins   Martin de Thurah / Chris Milk / Hideaki Motoki / Muto Musashi / ne-o / Pleix / Jonas Odell / +cruz / Ramon & Pedro / Vernie Yeung / Woof Wan-Bau

(01)

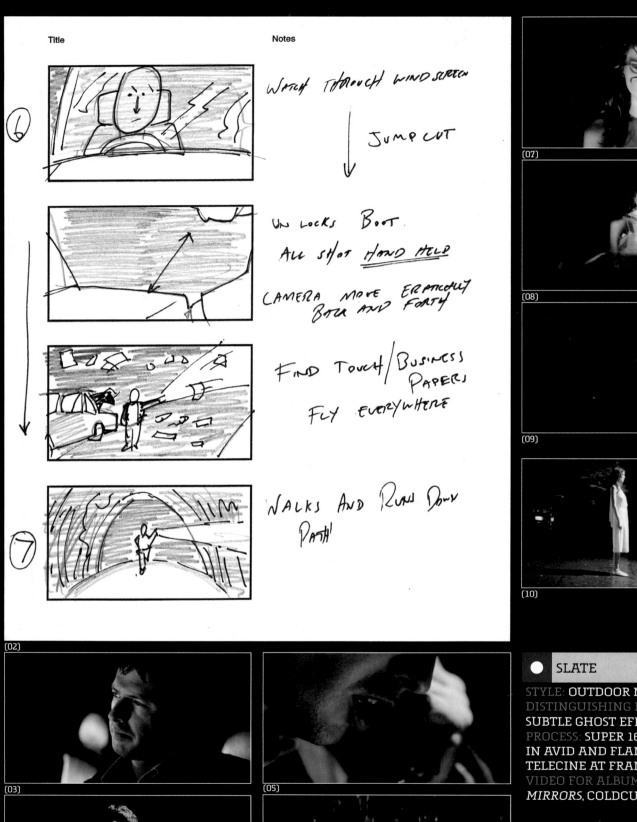

Title

Notes

WATCH THROUGH WINDSCREEN

JUMP CUT

UN LOCKS BOOT.
ALL SHOT HAND HELD

CAMERA MOVE ERATICALLY
BACK AND FORTH

FIND TOUCH/BUSINESS
PAPERS
FLY EVERYWHERE

WALKS AND RUN DOWN
PATH

(02)

(03)

(04)

(05)

(06)

(07)

(08)

(09)

(10)

● SLATE

STYLE: OUTDOOR NARRATIVE, FILM
DISTINGUISHING FEATURE:
SUBTLE GHOST EFFECTS, GRADING
PROCESS: SUPER 16MM. POSTED
IN AVID AND FLAME WITH
TELECINE AT FRAMESTORE
VIDEO FOR ALBUM: SOUND
MIRRORS, COLDCUT

❚❚

(01–02) Coldcut storyboards
(03–10) Video stills

Adam Levite AKA Associates in Science / Bessy & Combe / Brand New School   Ben Dawkins   Martin de Thurah / Chris Milk / Hideaki Motoki / Muto Musashi /ne-o / Pleix / Jonas Odell / +cruz / Ramon & Pedro / Vernie Yeung / Woof Wan-Bau

(01)

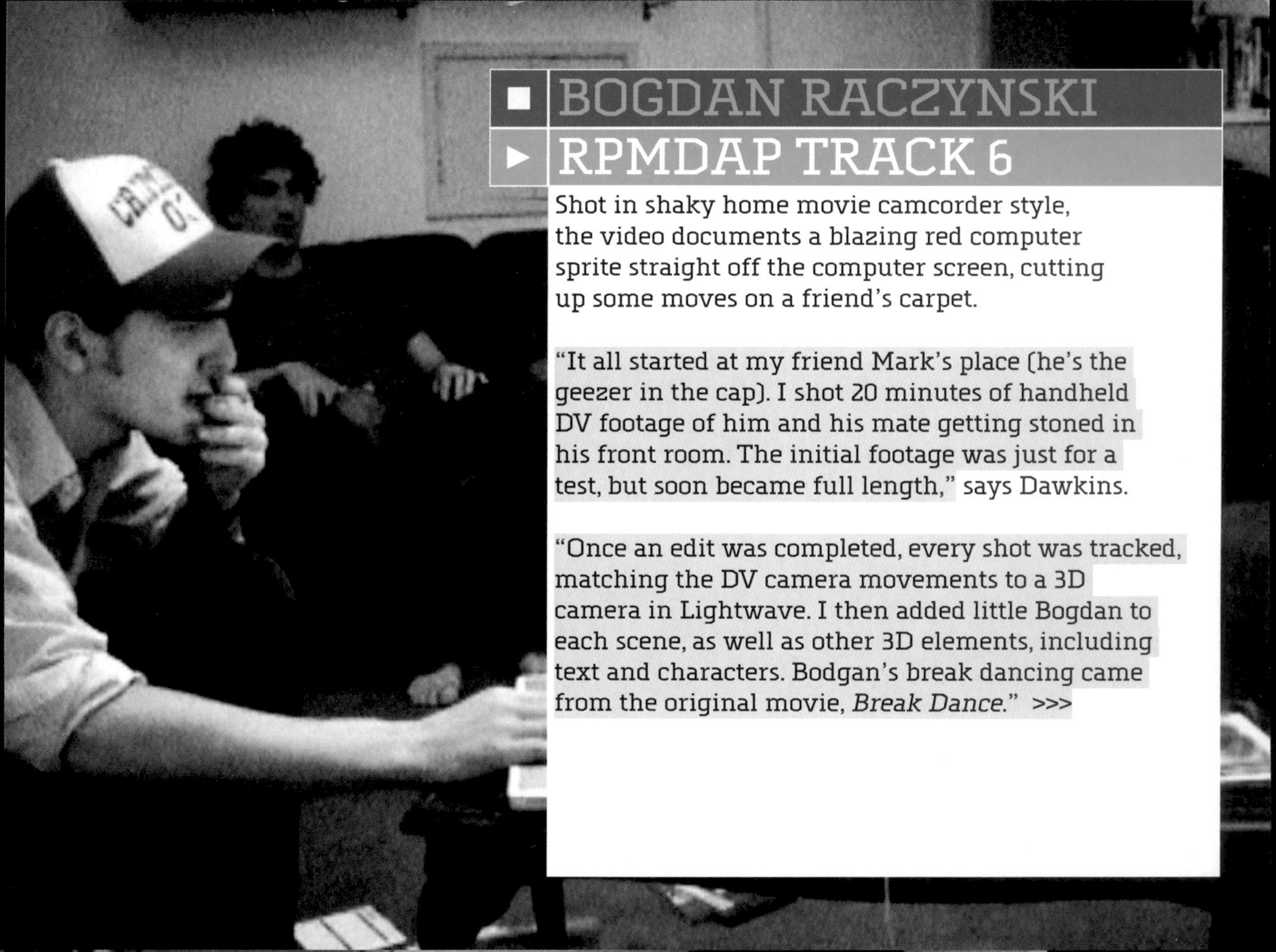

■ BOGDAN RACZYNSKI
▶ RPMDAP TRACK 6

Shot in shaky home movie camcorder style, the video documents a blazing red computer sprite straight off the computer screen, cutting up some moves on a friend's carpet.

"It all started at my friend Mark's place (he's the geezer in the cap). I shot 20 minutes of handheld DV footage of him and his mate getting stoned in his front room. The initial footage was just for a test, but soon became full length," says Dawkins.

"Once an edit was completed, every shot was tracked, matching the DV camera movements to a 3D camera in Lightwave. I then added little Bogdan to each scene, as well as other 3D elements, including text and characters. Bodgan's break dancing came from the original movie, *Break Dance*." >>>

(02)

(03)

(04)

(05)

(06)

(07)

(08)

(09)

(10)

(11)

(12)

(13)

(14)

● SLATE

STYLE: INDOOR LIVE ACTION/ANIMATION HYBRID
DISTINGUISHING FEATURE: DV FOOTAGE WITH
ARCADE SPRITE MOTION-MATCHING
PROCESS: MINI DV FOOTAGE SHOT THEN CUT ON PREMIERE.
AFTER EFFECTS, LIGHTWAVE, AND MATCH-MOVING
SOFTWARE WERE USED BEFORE AN AVID ONLINE
VIDEO FOR ALBUM: *RPMDAP (RENEGADE PLATINUM
MEGA DANCE ATTACK PARTY)*, BOGDAN RACZYNSKI

▮▮

(01–14) Motion matching a retro video sprite for
Bogdan Raczynski

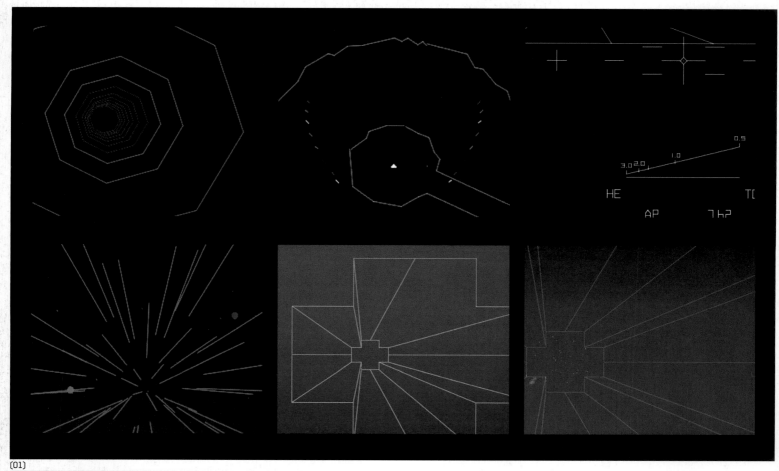

LITTLE THOUGHTS
► BLOC PARTY

The high-tech tools of Lightwave 3D and Flame in the current music video director's arsenal are used to emulate the retro feel of a state-of-the-art 1980s video. It makes this performance video leap out from the rest of the indie video pack.

"*Little Thoughts* was my first commercial music video. Bloc Party were relatively unheard of when I got the track in, and look at them now. The track had a great 1980s feel to it so I decided to base my idea on the videos of that era. It was a lot of fun researching. I remember showing the band Prince's video for *Alphabet Street* and saying, 'I wanna do that.'

"I shot the band against green and have done a wonderful job of 'badly' comping them with the blocky graphics which I made myself in Lightwave. I spent a day in Flame making it look as 'VHS' as possible." >>>

● SLATE

STYLE: GREEN SCREEN, BAND PERFORMANCE.
DISTINGUISHING FEATURE: 1980s PRIMARY-COLORED BLOCK GRAPHICS
PROCESS: DIGIBETA CAMERA
SOFTWARE USED: AFTER EFFECTS, LIGHTWAVE 3D, FLAME. CUT ON AVID
VIDEO FOR ALBUM: *SILENT ALARM*, BLOC PARTY

(01) Early background images
(02–11) Deliberately degraded video-like footage recreates the heyday of 1980s pop videos

(02)

(03)

(04)

(05)

(06)

(07)

(08)

(09)

(10)

(11)

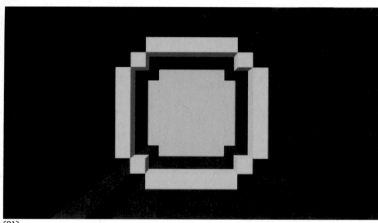

(01)

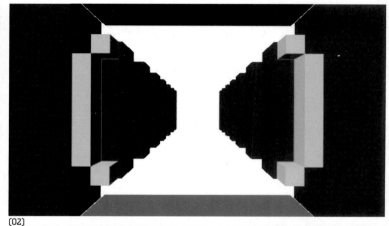

(02)

Treatment

For Bloc Party's 'Little Thoughts', I want to make a promo inspired by the golden age of music videos. A classic 1980s-style piece encompassing the techniques and technology of the time. I want the promo to house the analog video look of the era best illustrated by artists like The Jam, Talking Heads, Prince, and David Bowie.

This simple performance-based video will present the band playing against a white/bluescreen background, which will be later replaced by graphics. Using a mixture of both handheld and static shots, I want to recreate the techniques used at the time complete with a fast frantic edit that holds pace thoughout.

The white/bluescreen background will be replaced with simple graphics that will also work with the pace of the track. The graphics will enherit the eighties influence consisting of a mixture of Atari style blocks and simple wireframe 3D (there won't be any cheesey sound levels or graphic equalizers anywhere to be seen).

The background keying will be very rough leaving jagged pixels of blue around each member of the band. Other bright colors surrounding the band will bleed into one another with even brighter colors leaving light traces.

The whole piece will be shot on digibeta ensuring the classic video look, which can then be degraded further in post.

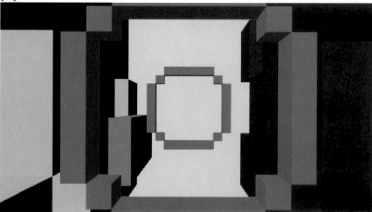

(03)

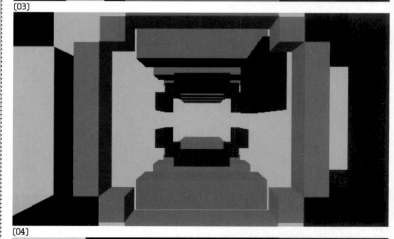

(04)

II

(01–05) Raw stills from background movie composite

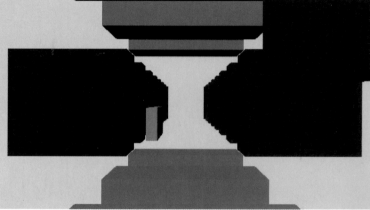

(05)

■ BREATHLESS
▶ NICK CAVE & THE BAD SEEDS

[01]

[02]

[04]

[03]

 ## SLATE

STYLE: INDOOR PERFORMANCE. ANIMATION
DISTINGUISHING FEATURE: DARK-SIDE DISNEY ANIMATION
PROCESS: SHOT ON HD AND DV CAMERAS. CUT ON AVID WITH TELECINE AT BLUE. USED PHOTOSHOP, AFTER EFFECTS, AND LIGHTWAVE 3D
VIDEO FOR ALBUM: *ABATTOIR BLUES/ THE LYRE OF ORPHEUS*, NICK CAVE & THE BAD SEEDS

An uneven video that comes across as either: A failure as either a performance or animated video; a joke resulting from a frustrated filming session; or a genius counterpoint to the usual look and feel of Nick Cave's other videos, depending on your viewpoint.

Dawkins filters Disney through *Watership Down*-style edginess, and Hayao Miyazaki-style cute animé. Cartoon rabbit plush dolls surround a barn (where the real band are performing), and claw themselves into reality, Roger Rabbit-style, to dance around Cave's feet.

"My original idea for this video was inspired by that great scene in *Mary Poppins* when Dick Van Dyke dances with the penguins. I wanted to shoot the band on a little set against a green screen, and then comp in the woodland environment around them. The animals would gather as the band play. Very zip-a-dee-doo-dah!

"The band refused to come down to a studio to shoot the scene, so I ended up writing a new location into the treatment. At the time, the band were practising in a barn near Heathrow. This became part of the idea and is featured in the video.

"We shot for two hours on HD cameras as the band performed the track. Using two cameras turned out to be extremely handy, too, as every time we pointed the camera at Nick, he faced away. The band performed the track six times before we had to leave. Four weeks later, I finished the animation. I'm attempting to complete a full-length animated version as we speak." ■

MARTIN DE THURAH

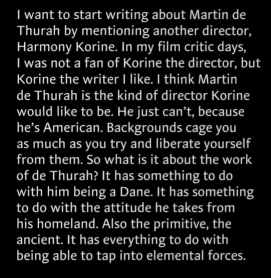

VIDEOGRAPHY

WHAT ELSE IS THERE?,	RÖYKSOPP
BULLETS,	EDITORS
SPECIAL,	MEW
IN PEAK FITNESS CONDITION,	SPLEEN UNITED
BEST DAY,	CARPARK NORTH
HUMAN,	CARPARK NORTH
PRE-EMPTIVE STROKE,	EPO-555K
LE BEAT'S ON FIRE,	EPO-555K
FÅGT OP I SKALLE,	MALK DE KOIJN
SÉANCE,	LISE WESTZYNTHIUS

I want to start writing about Martin de Thurah by mentioning another director, Harmony Korine. In my film critic days, I was not a fan of Korine the director, but Korine the writer I like. I think Martin de Thurah is the kind of director Korine would like to be. He just can't, because he's American. Backgrounds cage you as much as you try and liberate yourself from them. So what is it about the work of de Thurah? It has something to do with him being a Dane. It has something to do with the attitude he takes from his homeland. Also the primitive, the ancient. It has everything to do with being able to tap into elemental forces.

Completing six major music video clips in 2005, Martin de Thurah has been able to imbue the majority of these with real emotional power. He has created a series of capsule epics in an exceedingly short timeframe. Four-minute distillations of strange feelings. Complex, turbulent micro-narratives.

"I have elements I'm attracted to," states the director. "Things which come up every time I write or sit and scribble. Things like pine trees, simple houses, the feeling of being in exile in your own life. Heavy melancholy. Liquids coming out of people. The feeling of flying, and so forth. The complexity of things is something which is almost always there. I tend to make things complex in a simple way, because I think complexity is beautiful. I find life quite complicated—there is never just one version, there are loads of versions and layers in everything."

In a music video world where post-production wizardry has made everything more technical, because people are enamored by creating the fantastical, and drawn to the richly surreal, de Thurah brings everything back to its quintessence. To truth rather than artifice. He strips away those layers that aren't necessary.

"There are many ways ideas evolve," he explains. "I invent stories in different ways—and use different methods. When I started, I thought I should be clever but more and more I try *not* to be clever. It is a matter of being open, just taking what I have in front of me—a thought, a book, a word, all kinds of things. And I just write and write for some time."

On his work process: "I listen to the track on repeat for a while, but not too much—the mood and basic feel the track sets is important to find the right mental space for the video. When I find the right outgoing point, the main space, it has to sit deep in my stomach—then I write scenes. Sometimes I write them, others I draw them. It depends on the project. Then I rewrite and expand scenes, I cut the script down to maybe 20 percent of all notes I have been taking. I try hard to avoid being illustrative, which is difficult if the lyrics are not open.

"Sometimes, I get inspired by the lyrics, but often I feel that it's better that the video follows the song, not along the same track but on one that is parallel. For me, this expands the video. Illustrative videos are often dead. The space in between the song and the video needs to have some friction.

"I usually make storyboards myself, but more to nail down my own first feeling about how this scene should look, and to get an overview of the ingredients. Then I like to brainstorm a lot with the cinematographer, and for us to look in books together. It is so important to get on the same wavelength and feel. A hundred meetings later, we shoot the thing. Here I almost always only have time to shoot 75 percent of what I have planned—I need maybe 50 percent of my planned shots to actually make the video work—and I love the point of the shoot where I feel that now it is here. We landed the fish.

"When we edit, I often sit next to my editor and produce clips, and I start the post already here. I produce extra material, and play around with it—we put it in the edit and check it out. I have done a lot of post myself, which is an advantage when working on post-heavy productions—it makes my direction precise. I'm used to being very involved. This is a laboratory, the fun part. I create dummies and try a lot of directions out. After this, I pass it on to someone else, if it isn't already good enough."

De Thurah studied painting before graduating from the National Film School of Denmark, in Copenhagen, as an animation director, in 2002. His first videos involved more traditionally animated elements. In particular, *Fågt op i Skalle,* for Danish artist Malk de Koijn, carries with it a deceptively simple rendition, unembellished by overtly modern effects.

"I have been painting for quite some years, and the hours I have spent placing paint on canvas has shaped my eyes and my esthetics," explains de Thurah

His filmmaking comes alive in that liminal space that only a few directors can evoke. In his *What Else is There?* video for Röyksopp and *Human* promo for Carpark North, a young woman and a series of school-age chidren are imbued with extraordinary powers. Forces of nature are pushed to, and sometimes beyond, their limits. Within a few short seconds of watching each, we are transported to realities sliding silently next to our own but displaced. This is a sensation he likes to create: One where you are watching but you become lost for words because it feels so peculiar.

Martin de Thurah is a remarkable music video director because he captures the essences of things. Emotional spaces, liberated from rational explanation. He has a talent for creating imagery that rub up against the subconscious.

"I think music videos are a place where the film avant-garde is, so it's a very attractive window to sit in," enthuses the director. "Music videos have often blown me away and often, in the old days, I walked out of the living room inspired, with a smile on my lips, when someone had made something I never thought of. I really feel strongly for the exploration of the language."

I consider the future of the music video artform is held in the hands of artists like Martin de Thurah. It is such artists that make moving images so exciting and vital. His work holds truths that let us see beyond worldly things. >>>

Adam Levite AKA Associates in Science / Bessy & Combe / Brand New School / Ben Dawkins   Martin de Thurah   Chris Milk / Hideaki Motoki / Muto Musashi /ne-o / Pleix / Jonas Odell / +cruz / Ramon & Pedro / Vernie Yeung / Woof Wan-Bau

[01]

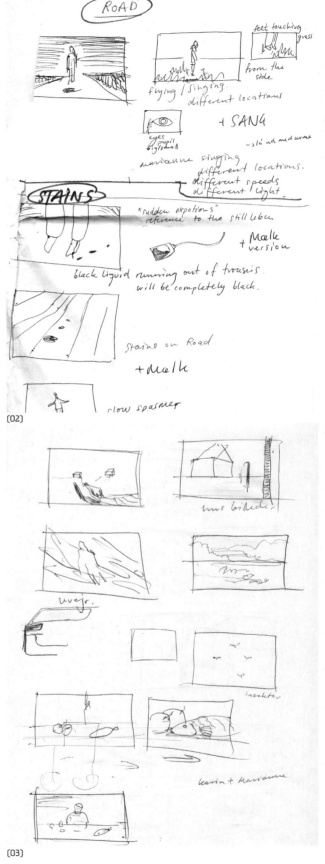

[02]

What Else is There? is a video that promises a glimpse into the profound, like much of de Thurah's work. A young woman floats through country roads, through a town; a milky substance dripping from her bare feet. A storm rages in the distance. Country houses hover, fragile, over the landscape, as if ready to disintegrate. Smoke emanates from holes in trees. A series of vignettes sees still-lifes that reference 17th-century painting, the graphic qualities of Danish painter, Wilhelm Hammershøj, and also of the young woman holding an older lady from a different time period (this is the track's actual vocalist, Karin Dreijer, of Swedish band The Knife).

Says de Thurah: "It all comes from a dream that is more abstract. It has no specific imagery, more an emotion, going through different mental states. In the dream, my aim is to keep myself straight. In a way, it's about focussing, avoiding disturbance. When I have the dream, it is always the same, and I always wake up happy." >>>

[03]

■

(01–03) Concept drawings and sketches for de Thurah's "dream state" video

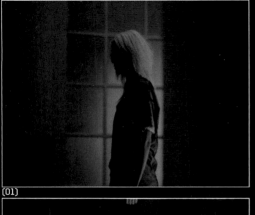

(01)

(02)

(03)

(04)

(05)

(06)

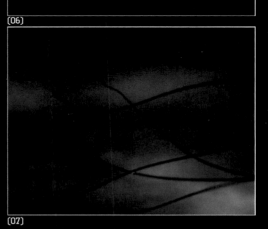

(07)

(08)

● SLATE

STYLE: DRAMATIC PERFORMANCE
DISTINGUISHING FEATURE: FLOATING
WOMAN AND BUILDINGS
PROCESS: SHOT ON 35MM FROM A
FIRE TRUCK. GREEN SCREEN SHOT
ON IMX, WITH ADDITIONAL DIGITAL
STILLS, AND MINIMAL DV FOOTAGE. 3D
ELEMENTS WERE MADE IN MAYA, XSI
& MAX, WITH A COMPOSITE MADE IN
SHAKE, AFTER EFFECTS, AND FLAME
VIDEO FOR ALBUM: *THE
UNDERSTANDING*, RÖYKSOPP

"The video woke up inside me between doing Mew and Editors. Between those videos, I was asked if I wanted to script on Röyksopp," says de Thurah. "They have a very strong video history, so it was a challenge to take up while lacking time. But I woke up clear one morning and sat down remembering my dream. Within two hours, I had written the script. It is the fastest I've written. Somehow, if you have less time, sometimes you become a lot better at writing a script. I don't have a formula. For me, these things are about how open you can write them. I want to write them quite open so I don't close too many doors in the beginning.

"Most of the time, I have a clearer idea of 'why?' and 'what?', but not with this video. This was my most abstract treatment by far. I needed to have another outgoing point. I like the ideas of place, the motion of floating, the idea you were moving through different places.

"Other ideas for the video included: Danish poet Tom Kristensen, who has written about a longing for shipwrecks and sudden death; for something wild to happen that shakes you so much that your house falls down and you have to start over. I wanted to get this tension, so it has distant thunderstorms, and little nightmarish elements, hints of decay." >>>

▌▌

(01-08) Skimming along the edge of reality, a woman drifts down a road and houses float over fields in *What Else Is There?*

(01)

(03)

(05)

(07)

(02)

(04)

(06)

(08)

Treatment

I'm inspired by some kind of weightlessness. A feeling of slow movement through the air. A memory we will fly through. I would like to cast a female to feature in the video.

She will be floating one meter above the ground, traveling throughout the whole video through different places at nighttime. The girl will be fixed in the picture, and the roads, landscapes, and spaces will move around her. We will see her float through empty houses, from different camera angles. It will be like an emotional journey, and yet I would like her to be a really modern person contrasting with the more dreamy universe she is traveling through. I would like the weather to change throughout the whole video, sometimes surrounding her—sometimes in the distance.

The style will be both modern (e.g.: she could be wearing jeans) and something inspired by old still-life paintings (with fruit, fish, and meat, but with a disturbing feel to it), and it will also have the sensitivity of some golden age paintings (see references).

imagination/reality
vpntetisk -legmar
masser af bagprojektioner

Membrane.

(09)

(01–08) On-set shots from *What Else Is There?*
(09) Notes on concepts and possible
visuals for the video
(10) Storyboard with detailed production notes

face
- varying light
fics with eyes
- flashlight in face
+ bright light behind her.

Marianne looks.

dog on road, Marianne

car passing

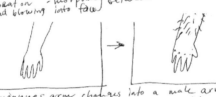

face with lot of
sweat on   - morphing between
- wind blowing into face

Mariannes arm changes into a male arm
- short flash (reference to "sudden explosion"

passes walking guy

Treatment

Examples of different scenes:

The girl will be floating down roads, through different landscapes, lip-synching.

The light will change on her face. Cars will pass her by. She will float past people walking down the road.

I would like the girl to be doing natural things at points as she floats, e.g.: brushing her hair.

We will see scenes in which she silently flies around empty houses, down the hallways, through living rooms—sometimes we will see people are sitting there.

A scene where the girl sits in a 'still-life'—like setting, eating a lot of fruit greedily. A girl is sitting at the end of the table eating as well. They look at each other.

In the end part, I would like old houses to silently float through landscapes (see an image I did with a house flying in the reference).

Please note: this is a rough idea and needs more development and refining.

Copyright © Martin de Thurah
@ Academy 2005

flying with sleeping lion
- thunder in horizon (p

face
- varying light
fics with eyes
- flashlight in face
+ bright light behind her.

hand shakes.

hand meets
other hand.

bigger shots
static camera
Marianne flying over containers?
car

face
- varying light
fics with eyes
- flashlight in face
+ bright light behind her.

Lots of light
- completely white appearing
- her from behind.

feet touching
grass

from the side

flying reading a book

black liquid

eyes
pupil
big/small

(10)

Adam Levite AKA Associates in Science / Bessy & Combe / Brand New School / Ben Dawkins / Martin de Thurah / Chris Milk / Hideaki Motoki / Muto Musashi / ne-o / Pleix / Jonas Odell / +cruz / Ramon & Pedro / Vernie Yeung / Woof Wan-Bau

(01)

(02)

■ HUMAN
► CARPARK NORTH

The director captures the burgeoning power of pre-teens growing into teenagers, as hormones rush through bodies, creating superhuman changes. The hormonal energy in the video is palpable. A cast of children stride down school corridors oozing attitude, breaking into jittery dances. Flailing, a girl runs in the gym, and she breaks free of earthly pull, into flight. A boy and girl run at each other, jump, and bounce off before touching, surrounded by invisible forcefields. These are the tangible barriers between the sexes about to be broken back down as relationships are reconfigured following injections of adrenalin, testosterone, and estrogen. With quick cuts of cells flowing through veins, clenched fingers, and hands, we are reminded of the emotional disturbances and changes of that period of youth.

(03)

(04)

(05)

(06)

(07)

(08)

(09)

(10)

(11)

(12)

"It was my idea and I put my focus on the pre-teenage period when your voice gets darker, your breasts start to grow, and so many things happen inside the body that you can't control," says de Thurah. "There is so much energy that wants to get out. You kick those you like and become very aware of yourself. And these kids are really strong, innocent, and fragile. It had to be strong in a human sense.

"I remember that I started feeling invisible, blending with the walls and the floor. I started daydreaming that I was flying—I wanted to fly, to be seen, and get others' attention, to suddenly exist. I guess I was invisible for quite a long time, and at the same time lot of things were going on inside me, with hair coming out of strange places.

"I found the kids for the video at different dance schools. I wanted them to be fragile and strong at the same time. This showed when I asked them to dance as 'ugly' as possible, like they were having electric shocks: Some kids wanted to look good, and tried to dance like Britney Spears—this was a no-go.

"We shot at my old childhood school, over two days. It was rock 'n' roll. I was working full time on some other project, so I had to make this in my spare time. There were many ideas I had storyboarded, but we only had time to do some of them. It was a quick process to make this little film—but really energetic." >>>

(01–12) The video captures the emotional and physical tension of puberty
(13) Many storyboarded scenes were cut due to time constraints
(14–20) On-set stills from the video, which was shot in two energetic days

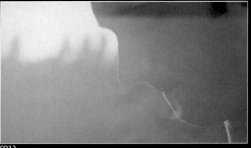

(01)

(02)

(03)

(04)

(05)

Shot on 16mm camera, this is a glorified outdoor performance video that presents a great attitude. Cars are wrecked and snatches of outdoor life are captured.

"I found that the song had this energy about attitude and confrontation," remembers de Thurah.
"I remembered a lot of identity issues—standing by the door in the living room, without any actual words on my tongue, but with a lot of unspoken feelings, looking at my father. There's so much energy inside—you might throw a hay bale in your friend's face, when you have restlessness in every pore."

(06)

(07)

❚❚

(01-07) Filmed in almost reportage-style naturalism, *Bullets* encapsulates the edgy urbanism of the Editors' sound

Adam Levite AKA Associates in Science / Bessy & Combe / Brand New School / Ben Dawkins / **Martin de Thurah** / Chris Milk / Hideaki Noroki / Muto Musashi / ne-o / Pleix / Jonas Odell / +cruz / Ramon & Pedro / Vernie Yeung / Woof Wan-Bau

● SLATE

STYLE: ORGANIC SYSTEMS
DISTINGUISHING FEATURE:
PICTUREBOOK-LIKE ANIMATION
PROCESS: DRAWN ON PAPER, COLORED IN
PHOTOSHOP, ANIMATED AND POSTED IN
AFTER EFFECTS, WITH 3D WORK IN MAYA.
VIDEO FOR ALBUM: *SNEGLZILLA*, MALK DE KOIJN

■ FÅGT OP I SKALLE
► MALK DE KOIJN

De Thurah: "The idea was to gather a turmoil of systems and connections between things, in the same way as the band writes the lyrics—build it up and break it down. It's not always clear what's going on, but the rhythm of the language and the way meaning is created was what I found interesting.

"The forest is the frame which makes a microcosm, in itself created of systems—both simple and complex. They merge into each other, influence, and change the other in a system of never-ending movement. We look upon these systems with the boy, and the point is to be taken away by the systems, be inside and experience them. Sometimes they make sense and sometimes the meaning is there without us seeing it." >>>

(01)

(02)

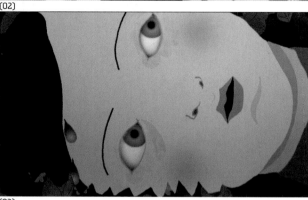

(03)

(04)

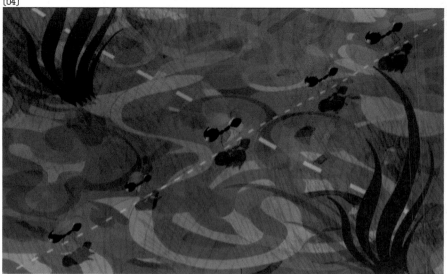

(05)

■

(01–05) The forest represents complex systems
and connections that the boy must untangle

[01]

[02]

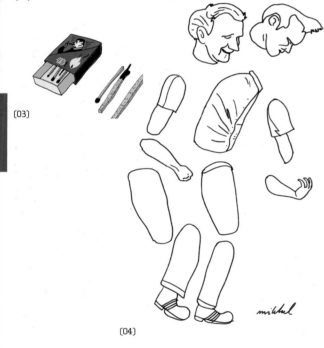

[03]

[04]

miktal

■ EPO-555K
► LE BEAT'S ON FIRE

"[This is] based on an old idea about a man burning his bridges, tearing his house down, and confronting his past with flames. Seeing his whole life—old postcards, photos of a girl he once loved—go up in flames. I wrote a page with one sentence scenes, and improvised some text," says de Thurah.

"We were in my apartment for one week. We worked all day and night, ate good food, and had lots of inspiring talks. One dogma was that we had to work fast, and therefore we should not refine anything. When a drawing was done, we had to use it. I wanted the video to have a rough feel. Mads, the character animator, invented a method of using Pythagoras to make the animations fast. It took him a day to find out, and after that he was flying."

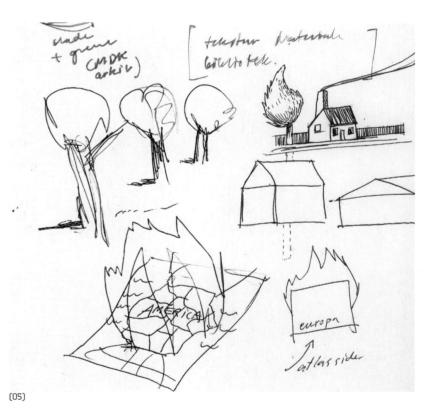

[05]

Treatment
(…)
A match.
A matchbox.
(…)
Afternoon, rough gray weather conditions.
A square, a triangle upon it, a house, 100 houses in the suburbs.
(…)
A man puts on rubber boots.
(…)
Arranges bonfire, attempts to light it up.
Sticks his rake into the fire…all old memories burn.

[06]

▌▌
(01–03) Animation produced using Pythagoras' theorem
(04–05) De Thurah did not allow his team to refine sketches
(06) A haiku-like treatment

[01–04]

SPECIAL
MEW

Shot in black and white, 35mm, with no effects. Edited with Avid DS. The clip was made on location in Sweden, and concerns a dramatic and mysterious conflict between a young man and a behatted femme.

De Thurah's concept: "I was inspired by the innocence in the first part of Ingmar Bergman's *Summer with Monica*, how pure love can look when you first experience it. So I wanted to make a dance with a man and a woman falling in love, make it weightless and passionate, and watch them fear and doubt it. In a way, this is a story about love when you are in your 30s and have experienced a few relationships die—about the darkness you see, the fears, and about being able to jump over the side and open up. It takes guts."

[05–08]

BEST DAY
CARPARK NORTH

Filmed on 16mm and 35mm camera, and posted with Maya and Avid DS. Locked-off shots of moonlight tracing shadows of trees, streetlights, building façades, and (presumably) band members. The video focusses on the strong faces of boys and girls in an attempt to look into their eyes, and decode their idea of their best day.

"This was a tricky one," admits de Thurah. "What is this feeling about 'the best day?' I wanted to create moments where time stands still and others where it moves—and capture little moments in young people's lives. Nothing wild needed to happen, I wanted it to be subtle."

[09–10]

IN PEAK FITNESS CONDITION
SPLEEN UNITED

De Thurah: "I shot this myself on a heat camera. The turnover was four days. A laboratory. A look upon different peaks. How it looks when the balloon bursts, when the muscles tighten or when you are in love and kiss passionately."

[11–14]

SÉANCE
LISE WESTZYNTHIUS

"Blood poisoning spreading in the veins of a girl. My first video ever," the director reminisces. ∎

(01) (02) (03) (04) (05) (06) (07) (08) (09) (10) (11) (12) (13) (14)

Adam Levite AKA Associates in Science / Bessy & Combe / Brand New School / Ben Dawkins / Martin de Thurah   Chris Milk   Hideaki Motoki / Muto Musashi /ne-o / Pleix / Jonas Odell / +cruz / Ramon & Pedro / Vernie Yeung / Woof Wan-Bau

CHRIS MILK

VIDEOGRAPHY

DOESN'T REMIND ME, AUDIOSLAVE
WALK TALL, JOHN MELLENCAMP
ALL FALLS DOWN, KANYE WEST
MONO, COURTNEY LOVE
JESUS WALKS, KANYE WEST
ROLLOVER DJ, JET
OCEAN BREATHES SALTY, MODEST MOUSE
THE GOLDEN PATH, THE CHEMICAL BROTHERS

"I've loved videos since I was a kid. I must have made a hundred *Thriller* videos in my backyard with my grandfather's VHS camera, and my brother and his friends dressed up as zombies."

Chris Milk's love of music and promos is infectious. When he gets a track to dream up a treatment on "I put it on my stereo on repeat. I jot down every bad idea that pops into my head. Eventually, something comes out that seems plausible. It may only be a scene, or a character, maybe just a shot. Then I start building around that."

The guy might actually be the Steven Spielberg of music video. There's nothing particular showy or overtly "auteurish" about his style, but he knows how to make videos that connect with people. Artists love him because he adds an extra dimension to the music without overpowering it.

"I really try and let the music and the narrative dictate the style," acknowledges the New York native. "I try to stay away from the idea of imposing a personal esthetic trademark on everything—that feels self-indulgent to me. You have to serve the story, not yourself. It's my job as the director to try and find the style that best complements the story. The story is always the most important thing, the style just frames it.

I think, if anything, my style and sensibility come through in the subject matter and the stories I choose to tell. I like things that are dark with some duality. Narrative is how I approach almost every track. It's not that I don't like performance videos; I just can't come up with any that I think will be compelling for four minutes. I wish I could, it would make my life so much easier. I over-compensate by writing over-complicated narratives."

These narratives range from the magic realism of *Ocean Breathes Salty* to more social commentary in the multi-award-winning *Jesus Walks* by Kanye West. Milk's early work was of the surreal and darkly fairytale, evident in videos for The Chemical Brothers and Courtney Love, respectively. Latterly, a more contemporary edge has entered into his finely crafted storytelling. *Jesus Walks* is far and away his most complex narrative with universal values. It reveals his expertise as an editor—a discipline he used to fund his education at the Academy of Art College in San Francisco's Film School.

"The message of the song, which becomes the subtext of the video, is that Jesus walks with everyone: Sinner, saint, murderer, drug dealer, it doesn't matter.

"So my idea was to take these morally reprehensible characters and carefully weave in Jesus and other biblical iconography into their stories to signify God is with them. The chain gang prisoner assumes the crucifix position when the guard is harassing him. Then the guard stabs him in his ribs with a baton like the Roman soldier did to Jesus. The drug smugglers' kilos of coke are transformed into doves; a modern miracle. The little girl rope-jumping wears wooden sandals. The KKK guy is dragging his burning cross up the mountain, as Jesus did the precursor to his crucifixion

"Kanye is performing in a room which transitions between hellish flames and the angelic halos of fluorescent light tubes on the ceiling. That section dives into the secondary theme of the duality of man; the idea that a person can be simultaneously both good and evil. Or, if you prefer, the more Christ-like notion of being both human and divine.

"Obviously, that's a lot to get into one video and I knew that much of it would be lost in the nature of its translation. The biggest concern I had—and Kanye as well—was tying a KKK guy into Jesus. That, suffice to say, is a little tricky in a hip-hop video. So far, no one has objected, though. In fact, some Christian groups have even sung the praises of the video's ultimately positive message."

Chris Milk sports a videography laden with awards, a testament to his gift for conveying subtle narrative layers in such a compressed and unforgiving time frame. With such old-fashioned values, why have I picked him as part of the vanguard, of the next-generation? Because he shows that stories can still win through, for his achievement in creating intelligent hip-hop videos in a sub-genre where bling has busted creativity for so long. And because, of the music video directors that have emerged on the scene in the last few years, Milk is the likeliest to succeed to the feature-length

"I'm looking for a special script that has so far proved elusive. I'm not interested in doing a movie just to do a movie. I want to do something unique, with teeth. I've had a number of offers, and read a hundred scripts, but I'd rather keep doing interesting music videos than do a sub par movie.

"If someone has even seen a video I've done, I'm excited, never mind if they've actually liked it. If I had to say one specific thing that seems to affect people, it's the use of narrative. But that is not any great creative leap on my part. Storytelling and storylistening is something that's ingrained in our DNA. Humans love stories. Beginning, middle, and end is universal. If you can pull it off in a four-minute music video, you are in pretty good shape." >>>

Adam Levite AKA Associates in Science / Bessy & Combe / Brand New School / Ben Dawkins / Martin de Thurah   Chris Milk   Hideaki Motoki / Muto Musashi /ne-o / Pleix / Jonas Odell /+cruz / Ramon & Pedro / Vernie Yeung / Woof Wan-Bau

JESUS WALKS
► KANYE WEST

Chris Milk argues that everyone has the power of redemption within them. *Jesus Walks* won Video of the Year at the 2005 BET Awards, and MTV Best Male Performance Video. Awash with biblical imagery and allusions to baptism and rebirth, the director managed to pull off the story without controversy, where lesser directors would have provoked a firestorm.

Says Milk: "I was very careful with the storyline. The way it is intended to translate is this: It is God that blows over the KKK guy's cross, causing it to roll down the mountain. The KKK guy's hate is so all-consuming that he tries to carry the physical manifestation of his hate back up the mountain for all to see. He is so blinded by that hate that he neglects to take into account the burning robe factor and gets into trouble. But God forgives him and causes it to rain, thereby extinguishing him. It's a baptism of sorts, washing away his sins. I doubt anyone got all that, but it's nice to at least make an attempt to build in some layers. The song is really powerful and deep so it sort of necessitates going the extra metaphorical step with everything." >>>

"READY!"

"BUM BUM BUM"

CHAINED FEET

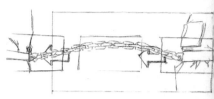
CHAIN GANG WALKS

KANYE WALKS FORWARD

CHAIN GANG AT WORK

DIGGING INTO ROCK

CHAIN GANG DIGGING

[04]

[01]

[02]

[03]

● SLATE

STYLE: NARRATIVE, PERFORMANCE
DISTINGUISHING FEATURE:
COMPLEX NARRATIVE
PROCESS: GRADED FILM WITH
PHOTOREALISTIC EFFECTS
VIDEO FOR ALBUM: *THE COLLEGE
DROPOUT*, KANYE WEST

(05)

(06)

(13)

(07)

(14)

(20)

(08)

(15)

(21)

(09)

(16)

(22)

(10)

(17)

(23)

(11)

(18)

(12)

(19)

(01–03) The chain gang is a departure from the urban gangs more often seen in hip-hop videos (04) Storyboards of the chain gang scene (05–23) A video with biblical undertones and drama

Adam Levite AKA Associates in Science / Bessy & Combe / Brand New School / Ben Dawkins / Martin de Thurah **Chris Milk** Hideaki Motoki / Muto Musashi / ne-o / Pleix / Jonas Odell / +cruz / Ramon & Pedro / Vernie Yeung / Woof Wan-Bau

MONO
▶ COURTNEY LOVE

In a leap of wild imagination, Princess Courtney is awakened in the nick of time, Snow White style, by a trio of fairies who rescue her from the evil paparazzi hordes.

"There is no specific artform or genre here," admits Milk. "I see little bits of things from all over creeping into my work. If I had to name something, I'd say a lot of it comes from childhood memories and traumas. Exorcising your demons through art can be very satisfying." >>>

● SLATE

STYLE: NARRATIVE
DISTINGUISHING FEATURE: DARK FAIRYTALE
PROCESS: FILMED LIVE ACTION WITH ANIMATED COMPOSITES
VIDEO FOR ALBUM: *AMERICA'S SWEETHEART*, COURTNEY LOVE

CU fairy flying [1 second]

More fairies join the flight path [7 seconds]

Fairies fly up to Courtney in a glass case [2 seconds]

Fairies fly around case [1 second]

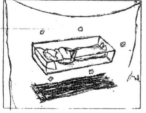
Fairies circle Courtney [1 1/2 seconds]

Single fairy weaves quickly through woods towards a distant glowing globe [6 seconds]

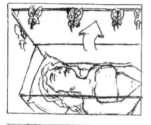
Fairies lift open top [2 seconds]

Fairies sprinkle fairy dust on Courtney [2 seconds]

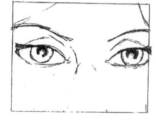
CU Courtney's eyes open [1 second]

Courtney sits up [2 seconds]

Courtney climbs out of case [2 seconds]

[01–02] Milk's detailed storyboarding technique
[03–20] Love's subverted Princess invades Middle America

(03)

(04)

(05)

(06)

(07)

(08)

(09)

(10)

(11)

(12)

(13)

(14)

(15)

(16)

(17)

(18)

(19)

(20)

(01)

(02)

(03)

(04)

Adam Levite AKA Associates in Science / Bessy & Combe / Brand New School / Ben Dawkins / Martin de Thurah / Chris Milk / Hideaki Motoki / Muto Musashi / ne-o / Pleix / Jonas Odell / +cruz / Ramon & Pedro / Vernie Yeung / Woof Wan-Bau

The video opens on our 21-year-old protagonist, Greg, walking into his office building. The year is somewhere in the late 1960s, early 1970s. He is dressed in the typical garb for the era: a brown suit in a questionable fabric with a fat tie. The film also has the feel of the period. It looks a little industrial, like grainy Kodachrome with saturated, muddy colors and a yellowish tint.

The interior of the office is rendered in a color palette of mustards, browns, and avocados. It's a pretty mundane place. Everyone is at least 15 years older than Greg. He ascends in the elevator under the soft buzzing glow of overhead fluorescents. He takes a moment to stare out the window as a flowered VW bus full of happy singing hippies passes by outside. His expression is one of numbed complacency. He punches his time card at the song's first cymbal crash.

This is the story of the one kid in the free love era who went and got a job in corporate America instead of rebelling against it. He chose the American dream, the supposed golden path of riches and power, over freedom and love.

THE GOLDEN PATH
► THE CHEMICAL BROTHERS

"I've been lucky that every commissioner I've worked with has been really supportive. Carol Burton-Fairbrother at Virgin UK will always have a special place in my heart for giving me my first music video, even though I didn't have a single clip on my reel," says Milk.

A 1960s office worker enters a psychedelic odyssey, all sparked by the magazine *News Makers* on his office cubicle desk with the coverline 'Free love.' Innocent period office accessories, such as a data-entry machine and photocopier, become gateways to another dimension of hippy liberation. >>>

(05)

(06)

(07)

(08)

(09)

(10)

(11)

(12)

(13)

(14)

(15)

● SLATE

STYLE: **NARRATIVE**
DISTINGUISHING FEATURE:
SURREAL 1960s STYLE
PROCESS: **FILMED WITH POST
PRODUCTION AND SPECIAL EFFECTS**
VIDEO FOR ALBUM: *SINGLES 93–03*,
THE CHEMICAL BROTHERS

❚❚
(01–15) Free love takes over the office
for The Chemical Brothers

Adam Levite AKA Associates in Science / Bessy & Combe / Brand New School / Ben Dawkins / Martin de Thurah | Chris Milk | Hideaki Motoki / Muto Musashi /ne-o / Pleix / Jonas Odell / +cruz / Ramon & Pedro / Vernie Yeung / Woof Wan-Bau

(01)

(02)

(03)

(04)

(05)

(06)

(07)

(08)

(09)

(10)

(11)

(12)

■ ALL FALLS DOWN
► KANYE WEST

Chris Milk's most obviously technical video employs a point-of-view shot of Kanye West's character escorting his girl to the airport while expounding on a life of transience and excess.

"I get the most questions about the POV reflections in Kanye West's *All Falls Down*. The simple explanation is that there is a layer filmed for his POV, a layer for the image being reflected, and a layer of his hands in front of green screen to match his hands in the reflection," explains Milk.

"Obviously if you are shooting into a mirror, you are looking at yourself with the camera, so I knew I would shoot the image in the mirror as a separate layer. That was the easy part. By far the hardest was figuring out how to get the subtle motion and rotation in each layer to work together so it seemed like one cohesive POV. For instance, when Kanye's reflection turns his head in the mirror, his POV has to rotate accordingly. If the motion and rotation don't match, layer to layer, they look like they're floating independently in space and the effect is completely lost.

"We did quite a number of tests on video first before we ever shot a frame of film. And, truthfully, I still don't think it's absolutely perfect. Because of time constraints, I only got to shoot two takes of each layer. If you look at the foreground hands, there are a couple of moments when they don't match the reflection perfectly." >>>

‖ (01–12) Milk's video for Kanye West is a technical tour de force with one continuous point-of-view shot sustained throughout the clip

(01)

(02)

(03)

(04)

(05)

(06)

(07)

(08)

(09)

(10)

(11)

(12)

(13)

(01–05)

DOESN'T REMIND ME
AUDIOSLAVE

"Audioslave is probably what I'm most happy with," says Milk. It's a capsule narrative social document of a boy growing up and dealing with an absent father (a military man). Uncle Sam's American dream turns sour in Milk's anti-war ode against invasion and parental loss.

(06–10)

OCEAN BREATHES SALTY
MODEST MOUSE

Childhood magic realism, as a boy rescues a scarecrow from a rapeseed field and learns about the afterlife.

(11–13)

WALK TALL
JOHN MELLENCAMP

A period piece against prejudice. Filmed mainly in a black-and-white, high-contrast style, a dwarfish milkman must escape the lynch mobs to be with his wheelchair-bound sweetheart. John Mellencamp in melodramatic form. ■

HIDEAKI MOTOKI

Hideaki Motoki's animation is precise, technical, and beautiful 3D. It doesn't try to hide its artificiality. His work contains no modish motion graphics trickery. No compositing or photorealistic effects. It is free of any hybrid live action. It glories in being able to imagine and create anything from the computer screen. The fact that the director has decided to take this into a figurative rather than abstract direction places him outside the artistic stream of contemporaries.

"My own style? I call it 'Hear vision, see music.' That is the theme," Motoki explains. "My aim is to think and create a world with my own hands that I have never seen before and would like to see."

This urge drew him inexorably to creating his own visual works, although initially he was heading in quite a separate direction. "I was studying for a degree in law, but my interests were completely different at that time. My first work presentation belonged to media art, and was an installation with 'computer and unconsciousness' as the theme.

"After that, I built up my career by being involved in producing games with themes around the human body and life. I gradually developed a strong craving to create my own visual work instead of doing joint projects, and started *Zounds*."

Zounds showcases a fantastically rendered collection of imaginative musical creatures, illustrations of his primary animation influence: "The movements and shapes of various living creatures, which I encountered on the beach as I was growing up by the sea."

These characterizations could only have been conceived in Japan. They are pure eye candy, original, and quirky. They eschew dominant Japanese animation styles seen in animé and computer-gaming. They exhibit "kawaii," a quality of cuteness also prevalent in the super-deformed style of that visual culture, and at the same time a futurism that the super-deformed does not contain.

"My own style? I call it 'Hear vision, see music.' My aim is to think and create a world with my own hands that I have never seen before and would like to see" HIDEAKI MOTOKI

Zounds' originality was noticed by Rays and the label asked him to produce a piece for their *Moonflowers* release.

So, what is his process of creation when it comes to the music video clip? "First, I incorporate my own interpretations, I associate ideas freely to broaden the world of the piece of music more. Then, I collect the fragments of ideas produced from there, relate them, distribute them on the time axis to set out an outline. Ideas that emerge during production—an important step—are added to these, leading to the completion of the project."

Creating the virtual models and worlds of the director's work is a painstaking and laborious process. 2005's *Churazima* is his most intricate and ambitious work so far. "This music piece's theme is Japan's most southern island, Okinawa—a beautiful island. This collaboration with Ryukyudisko began by them sending me an unfinished rough track, since a good amount of time was necessary to make a full CG image of the rich, glaring, primary-colored world.

"Following that, 3D modelling and idea brainstorming proceeded, then a tight schedule of animation work began on completion of the music piece. During production, my focus was on the idea of the Ryukyudisko logo representing the island's shape, characters vividly running around the island, and the best way of bringing them and the music together."

All Motoki's creations are character-led, and this interest can be seen in the cited inspirations and influences behind his work: Takashi Nemoto, the underground manga artist and leading exponent of outsider comics art in Japan; avant-garde artist Taro Okamoto, from the fine art world, who produces simple sculptural forms resembling primitive geometric and organic characters; and Shigeru Mizuki, a household name in Japan, the massively famous cartoon artist of the *GeGeGe no Kitaro* manga and animation series.

Like Mizuki, who can take credit for breathing a "humane" edge and an extra dimension into the grotesque world of "yokai"—Japanese goblins—Motoki injects a warmth into the cold artificiality of virtual characters. Sometimes this results in the uneasy sensation of the "Uncanny Valley." Coined by Japanese roboticist Masahiro Mori, this theory relates to our emotional unease associated with robots (or other non-human entities such as CG characters) when their representation becomes "almost human" but the imitation is not yet perfect enough to completely deceive us. It's a feeling I get watching *Moonflowers*, whose protagonist could be seen as some kind of benevolent, futuristic yokai, but not when I watch the exotic dragons of *Churazima*, or musical insectoids of *Zounds*.

"I cannot make a sweeping generalization, but I think European and American music videos are dynamic and energetic, and many Japanese ones are delicate," states the director. I hope Hideaki Motoki continues to pursue that imbalance and delicacy within his work. >>>

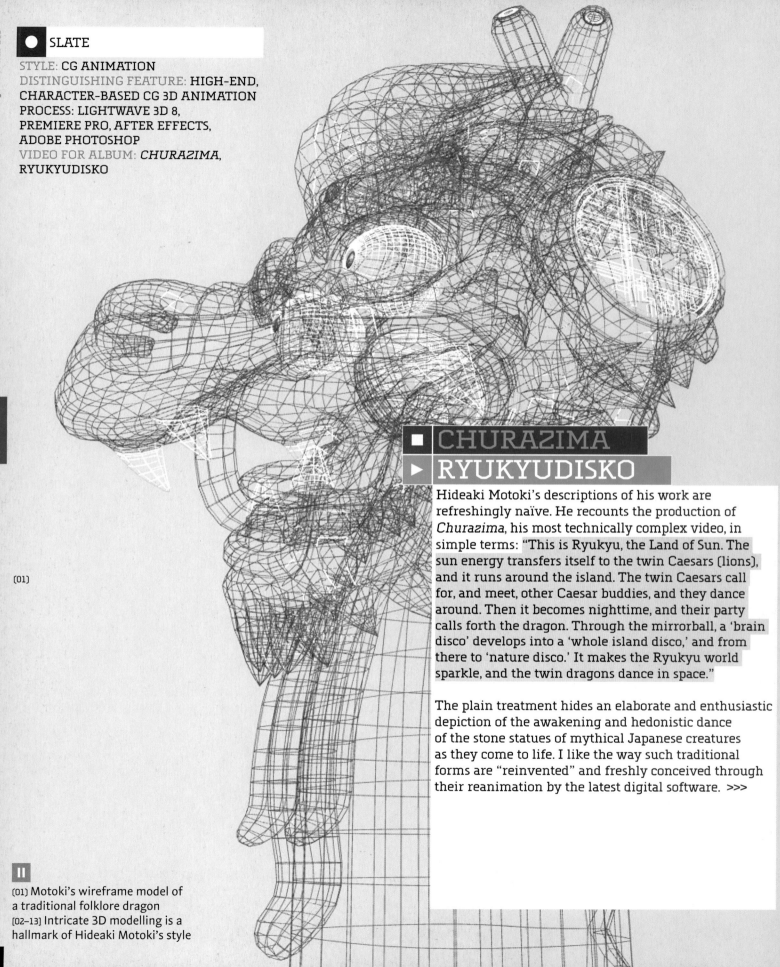

● SLATE

STYLE: CG ANIMATION
DISTINGUISHING FEATURE: HIGH-END,
CHARACTER-BASED CG 3D ANIMATION
PROCESS: LIGHTWAVE 3D 8,
PREMIERE PRO, AFTER EFFECTS,
ADOBE PHOTOSHOP
VIDEO FOR ALBUM: *CHURAZIMA*,
RYUKYUDISKO

[01]

■ CHURAZIMA
▶ RYUKYUDISKO

Hideaki Motoki's descriptions of his work are refreshingly naïve. He recounts the production of *Churazima*, his most technically complex video, in simple terms: "This is Ryukyu, the Land of Sun. The sun energy transfers itself to the twin Caesars (lions), and it runs around the island. The twin Caesars call for, and meet, other Caesar buddies, and they dance around. Then it becomes nighttime, and their party calls forth the dragon. Through the mirrorball, a 'brain disco' develops into a 'whole island disco,' and from there to 'nature disco.' It makes the Ryukyu world sparkle, and the twin dragons dance in space."

The plain treatment hides an elaborate and enthusiastic depiction of the awakening and hedonistic dance of the stone statues of mythical Japanese creatures as they come to life. I like the way such traditional forms are "reinvented" and freshly conceived through their reanimation by the latest digital software. >>>

■
[01] Motoki's wireframe model of a traditional folklore dragon
[02–13] Intricate 3D modelling is a hallmark of Hideaki Motoki's style

86

[02]

[03]

[04]

[05]

[06]

[07]

[08]

[09]

[10]

[11]

[12]

[13]

ZOUNDS
▶ MATSUMAE

Motoki: "A project with the 'ecosystem of sound' as its theme. It features Zounds—instrument creatures—communicating through sounds, creating various sounds of emotion by contacting other Zounds and their environment, and explores their development and evolution."

Zounds is a personal project initiated by the director. The uniquely designed characters act as instruments in their own musical world, that has its own fully formed internal logic. With a restricted color palette, ultra-clean lines, and immediately winning characterization, Motoki's development of this project is intriguing and could be a welcome extension to the music video form with international appeal. >>>

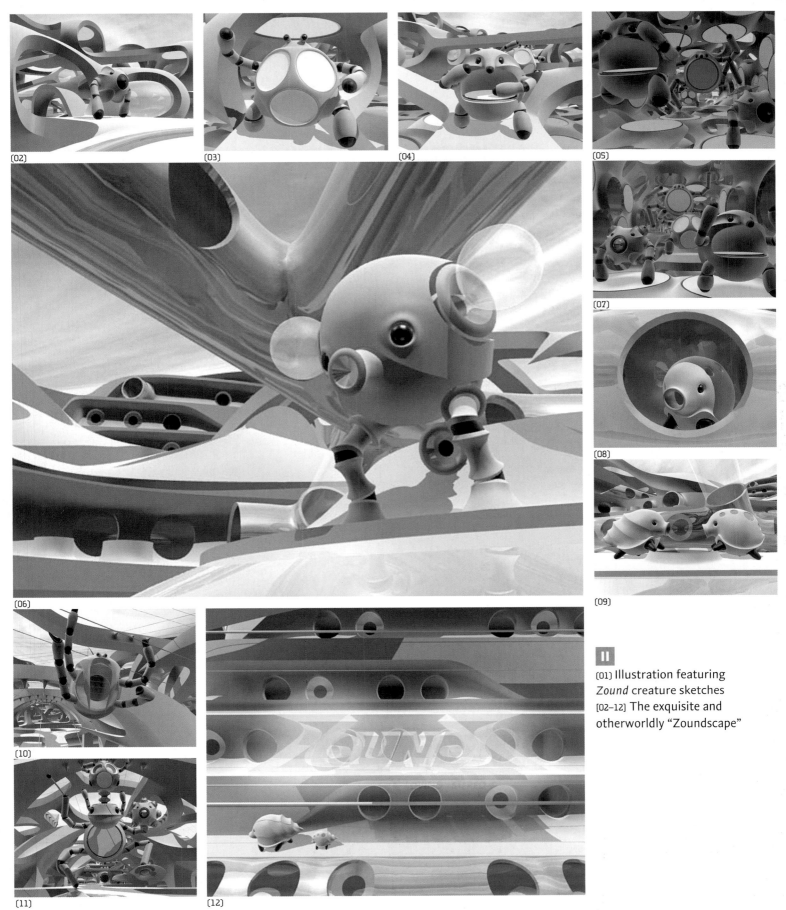

(02)

(03)

(04)

(05)

(06)

(07)

(08)

(09)

(10)

(11)

(12)

II

(01) Illustration featuring *Zound* creature sketches
(02–12) The exquisite and otherworldly "Zoundscape"

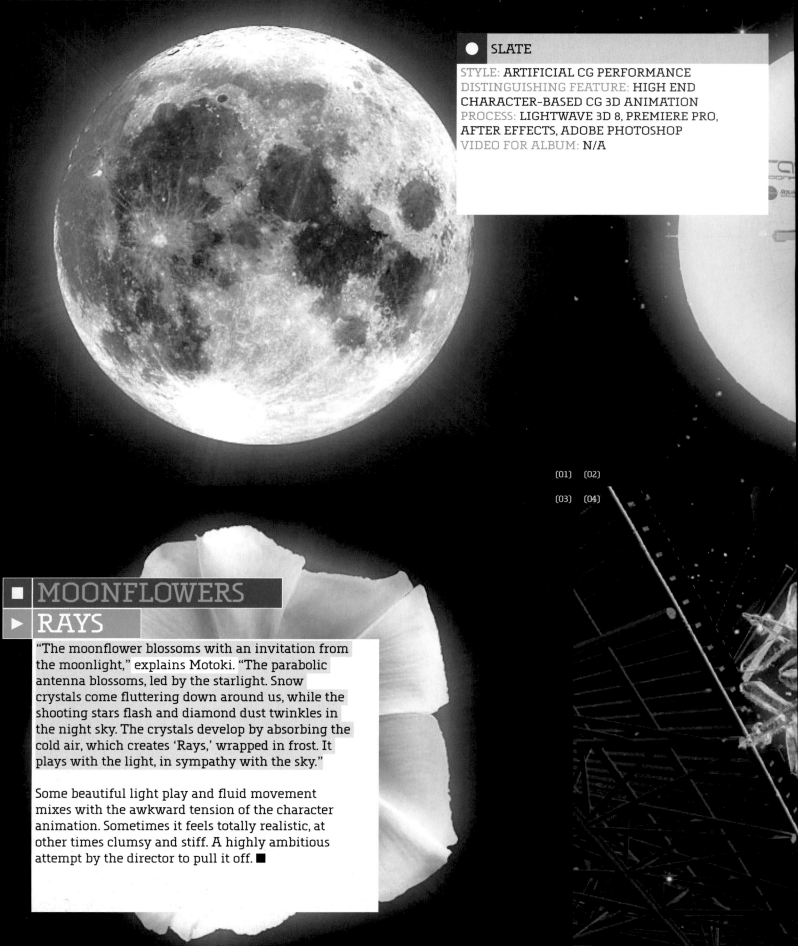

● SLATE

STYLE: ARTIFICIAL CG PERFORMANCE
DISTINGUISHING FEATURE: HIGH END
CHARACTER-BASED CG 3D ANIMATION
PROCESS: LIGHTWAVE 3D 8, PREMIERE PRO,
AFTER EFFECTS, ADOBE PHOTOSHOP
VIDEO FOR ALBUM: N/A

(01) (02)

(03) (04)

■ MOONFLOWERS
▶ RAYS

"The moonflower blossoms with an invitation from the moonlight," explains Motoki. "The parabolic antenna blossoms, led by the starlight. Snow crystals come fluttering down around us, while the shooting stars flash and diamond dust twinkles in the night sky. The crystals develop by absorbing the cold air, which creates 'Rays,' wrapped in frost. It plays with the light, in sympathy with the sky."

Some beautiful light play and fluid movement mixes with the awkward tension of the character animation. Sometimes it feels totally realistic, at other times clumsy and stiff. A highly ambitious attempt by the director to pull it off. ■

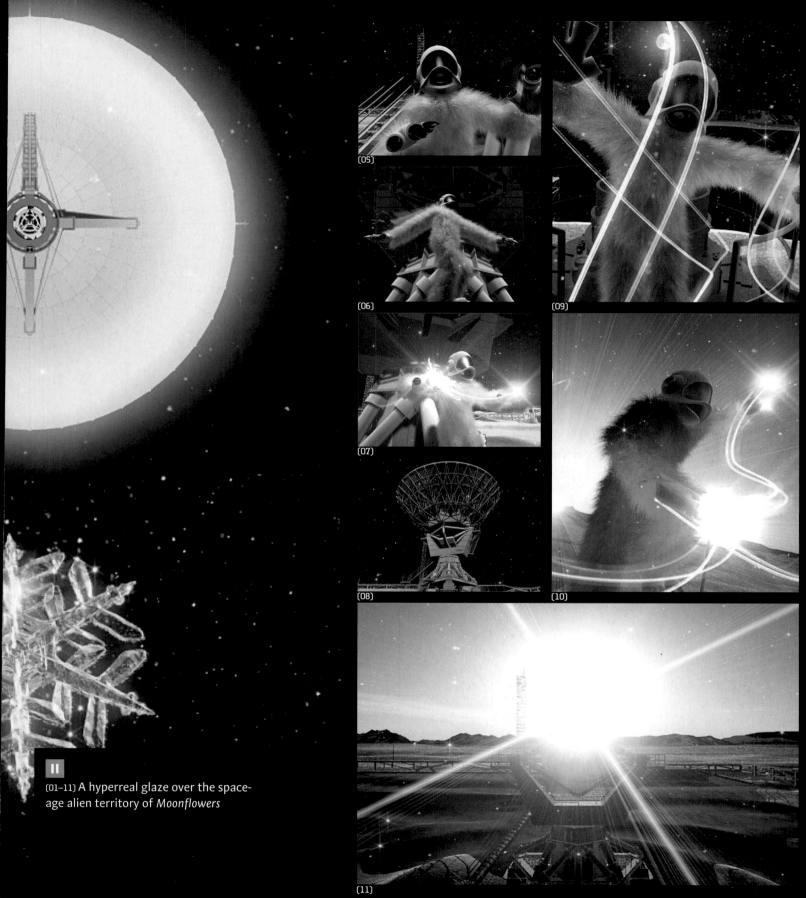

(05)

(06)

(07)

(08)

(09)

(10)

(11)

II

(01–11) A hyperreal glaze over the space-age alien territory of *Moonflowers*

Adam Levite AKA Associates in Science / Bessy & Combe / Brand New School / Ben Dawkins / Martin de Thurah / Chris Milk / Hideaki Motoki Muto Masashi ne-o / Pleix / Jonas Odell / +cruz / Ramon & Pedro / Vernie Yeung / Woof Wan-Bau

MUTO MASASHI

Maybe it is something to do with feeling embattled in a foreign place, or a need to regard or protect foreign bodies, but Japanese director Muto Masashi has made an instantly recognizable device of obsessively encircling the artists or characters he films within his music video work. It is as if he is drawing a barrier around them, making them otherworldly—separating them from us; fiction from reality.

In a way, Muto Masashi is an odd choice for a book ostensibly about the next generation of music video directors. After all, he has been directing since 1986. But it is in the fact his European directorial career wasn't "born" until 2002, with a promotional video for Frou Frou, that makes him eligible for this book. These different timelines make his approach different to many other contemporary directors who have come from backgrounds filled with the latest software tools, and steeped in new disciplines such as motion graphics and digital illustration. His process and approach diverge from the rest.

"I would have liked to say I am familiar with graphics," states Masashi. "I sometimes take photographs for advertisements or my own pleasure, but I am not a photographer. Since I was originally dealing with fashion, I was influenced by fashion photography and photographers."

At one time, music video's directorial ranks were filled by photographers turning to film. Currently, this trend has been overpowered by that of the motion designer with their graphic sensibilities. Masashi's entrance to directing was through another alternate route, designing the visuals for the catwalk shows of legendary fashion designers.

"At the time I was involved, it was the golden age for designers. There was Rei Kawakubo of Comme des Garçons, and Issey Miyake, for example," remembers Masashi. He created intense imagery to complement both designers' collections. "They were exceptionally particular about their work," he observes, "whereas musicians are more laid-back.

"The company that I started working at was dealing with fashion videos by chance. It represented 80 to 90 percent of work there. With promos, advertising effect is necessary, hence the music. How to present the artist becomes an important point. On the other hand, fashion videos are like art: Visualizing the image according to the clothes' themes defined by designers. To that extent, it is a presentation of the clothes, but less commercialized— it feels like painting a picture."

"My intent is to adapt time, and work out how to incorporate it with my esthetic sense" MUTO MASASHI

This background goes some way to explaining Masashi's manner, the way the director specifically treats his camera. It is aggressively inquisitive. Relentlessly, it searches for the perfect frame, like the artist's brush, or the photographer's lens.

"My intent is to adapt time, and work out how to incorporate it with my esthetic sense," he says. It is like he has to interpolate time around these specific moments, and has developed techniques to aid him in this, such as his signature ringing movement. How did that first come about? "I wanted to create a delicious look for a Japanese rock band because they were singing about drugs, so I asked the SFX team to make a machine that does this fast rotation."

Masashi is just as matter of fact about why he began directing in Europe: "Imogen Heap from Frou Frou saw me in *Nylon* and *i-D*, and she asked me to do her video. That's how I started."

It is more insightful hearing the differences he observes between the separate regions. After all, besides his fashion background, Masashi's other anomaly is that he is one of the few Japanese directors working in Europe with European artists.

"In Japan, I get asked to do a promo directly from the labels' A&R. There is no marketing division to think about creating a decent campaign strategy to help develop their artists in Japan. So when I get jobs, I am pretty much free to do whatever I want visually. It is a part of my job to think of how they should look. But in Europe or the US, marketing people and commissioners have a lot of control over the video. It's efficient, I think. There is no comparable position to the video commissioner in Japan."

It was the video for the Death in Vegas track *Scorpio Rising* that cemented Masashi's reputation in Europe.

"I always wanted to do an historical theme, and they wanted me to write historically," he recalls. "I was excited. I tried to create a mismatch between Japanese tradition and cool modern Western music."

The unanchored feeling this Asian director brings to European work gives it a feeling of what French philosopher Jean Baudrillard termed the "hyperreal." This overpowering emotion of the "simulated," his fetishization, revisitation, and perfection of one technique, sets arch-stylist Masashi apart from the roving attention other directors display. >>>

(01)

(03)

(02)

(04)

■ SCORPIO RISING
▶ DEATH IN VEGAS

One of the most powerful of recent videos, *Scorpio Rising*'s enduring appeal lies in the tension between the electroclash, ultra-contemporary sound of the track against a vision of a reimagined Samurai-era Edo. Masashi has reduced Western notions of Bushido period Japan to lacquer-armored assassins, women being painted by master calligraphers, temples, and warrior stand-offs on windswept streets between low-rise wooden buildings. A series of action vignettes fetishize the glint of katana, the red wash of death blows.

Masashi: "We were short on budget, and daylight hours were short because it was a winter filming, so shooting time was limited. To be honest, it is surprising that we were able to shoot such an amount. There was not enough budget for rehearsal either, so just a bit of practising the day before with the models." >>>

(05)

● SLATE

STYLE: PERIOD DRAMA
DISTINGUISHING FEATURE:
SAMURAI WARRIORS IN REVOLUTION
PROCESS: FILM WITH POST PRODUCTION,
USING FLAME AND INFERNO
VIDEO FOR ALBUM: *SCORPIO
RISING*, DEATH IN VEGAS

(06)

(07)

(08)

(09)

(10)

(11)

(12)

(13)

(14)

(15)

(16)

(17)

(18)

(19)

(01–19) The highly stylized imagery and costumes of *Scorpio Rising* illustrate Musashi's background in creating moving images for fashion designers' catwalk shows

(01)

(03)

(02)

(04)

NO ORDINARY PAIN
▶ NINA JAYNE

Day transforms to night in a series of revolutions outside Tokyo's super-modern Ueno Station plaza. Commuters and rioters leave motion trails as the singer segues seamlessly from nightclub to city street, then to an opulent Japanese room. Masashi is showboating, playing around with locative and temporal disjoint: "It was deadly hot during filming. I was concerned about producing the artificial aspects, but that was it. It felt the same as usual, as it was shot in Japan."

(05)

(09)

(06)

(10)

(07)

(11)

● SLATE

STYLE: CONTEMPORARY PERFORMANCE
DISTINGUISHING FEATURE: REVOLUTION
ON TOKYO STREETS
PROCESS: FILM WITH POST PRODUCTION,
USING FLAME AND INFERNO
VIDEO FOR ALBUM: *FOUND MY PLACE*, NINA JAYNE

(08)

(12)

(13)

(15)

(14)

(16)

(17)

[01–17] Muto Musashi typically employs imagery of high dynamic range (HDR) offering an ultra-real, ultra-clear rendering of reality

(01)

(05)

(02)

(06)

(03)

(07)

(04)

(08)

(01–08)

MUST BE DREAMING
FROU FROU

Using a simple set of locations—a long, light-green corridor, a darkened room, and a room where the vocalist is plunged and enveloped in blue water—Masashi evokes a dreamy feeling, unselfconsciously free of meaning and context. The camera whip shifts between the spaces and angles to keep the singer in focus.

Masashi says, "The interest and the difficulties in this video were almost the same. There were technical difficulties, such as extending the corridor without CG, hair not floating well under the water, and the like. Also it was my first work outside Japan and I experienced a sense of unity with the UK staff. Usually when I work abroad, I feel like a guest."

(01)

(02)

(01–06)

MISS U LESS, SEE U MORE
FAITHLESS

A more spiritual video, themed with spirits and ghosts flowing in and out of bodily experience. Monks dance shamanically. A golden Buddha awakens. This video effectively uses the director's trademark techniques to give them more narrative meaning. His use of layered imagery, ghosting, and trails making sense of a spiritual awakening.

"It breaks my heart that it was not aired," says the director. "The CG did not make it, and the final pictures were unable to meet the demands of the record company. It was quite a shock, since we put in a great effort shooting it during the approach of a hurricane."

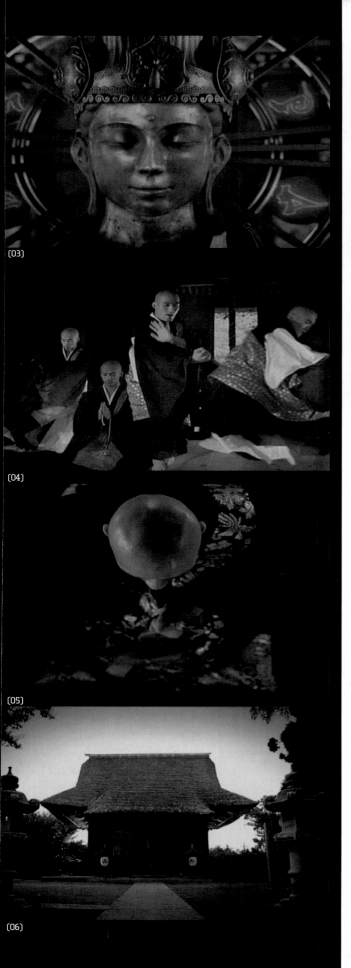

(03)

(04)

(05)

(06)

(01)

(02)

(03)

(01–03)

JUMPIN'

LIBERTY X

A manufactured pop group are laced with familiar abstracted glamor, their performance haloed on a blinding white dancefloor by a shimmering chandelier.

"I was unlucky with staff," recalls Masashi. "The situation was difficult, with plans not running smoothly, being cancelled without notice, and such. The special machine parts brought from Japan broke down during construction due to transportation and reassembly. Fortunately, I knew someone who was coming over to London the following day for my commercial work, so he brought a spare machine part. This work was all done in London. The laid-back style of working was interesting."

(01)

(02)

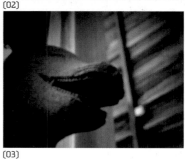

(03)

(01–03)

SONY PLAYSTATION

An unsettling spot for PlayStation, presented with *Ringu*-like horror tension. It's a surreal montage of free-flowing imagery. The camera moves through eerie timber square frames up an abandoned country path. We see a distorted face and eyes in an automobile mirror, a toy drummer, the yin and yang symbol, and Swiss clocks. A white-bandaged and bloodied figure floats through a corridor of flying flowers. Above, we see speeded-up, gray storm clouds. A surreal spectacle. ■

ne-o

Adam Levite AKA Associates in Science / Bessy & Combe / Brand New School / Ben Dawkins / Martin de Thurah / Chris Milk / Hideaki Motoki / Muto Musashi   ne-o   Pleix / Jonas Odell / +cruz / Ramon & Pedro / Vernie Yeung / Woof Wan-Bau

VIDEOGRAPHY

THE BOXER, **THE CHEMICAL BROTHERS**
VISIONARY WORLD, **KEN ISHII**
STORYBOARD, **MIHO**
LATE AT NIGHT, **FUTURESHOCK**
ME AND MADONNA, **BLACK STROBE**

ne-o have got a very modish Anglo-Japanese thing going on, even if they are at pains to downplay it. They downplay "everything." It's part of what makes their material, their music videos, so distinctive. Jake Knight and Ryoko Tanaka are both personal and professional partners. They've been playing with spatio-temporal tricks for years. It comes naturally. For example, whenever I bumped into Knight at an event when I was living in London, it was always with a start that I saw him. He slips in and out of space. Like his work.

I've a long history with ne-o, commissioning an early short, *b3*, and producing another short film, *Salaryman6*, with them. Both films are a true reflection of their uncompromising vision of architectural exploration. Whereas Michel Gondry is playful with space, and Jonathan Glazer is master of using it to hook on an epic scenario, ne-o are indicative of the "next generation," in that their investigations are more formal and scientific. From the personal films through to the music videos, space is interrogated, pushed to—and beyond—the physical limits. They use space more than sound to trigger ideas.

"In music video, you get a track which starts you off. I purposely don't get really into the track, or overplay it," elucidates Knight. "I want to get just an impression of a track. We forget about it for a bit then, come up with ideas. It's quite hands-off: We just check it out at the beginning of the creative process, to see whether it's obvious if it needs a slow feel, for example."

They brainstorm through the process using books and objects, then analyze it through a head-to-head in a random space outside of their studio. Knight explains that they want to go somewhere low pressure, with little visual impact, so they can let the random triggers and inspirations come to the fore.

"A lot of that technique thing comes from not having the facility
or know-how to do exactly what you want. So you do it and it
creates an approximation of what you wanted initially. It's a
kind of DIY-thing with crusty edges and stuff" JAKE KNIGHT

Knight: "We used to go to Stansted airport. It has nice acoustics which makes it feel like a library. It has got that sort of dead feeling about it. A few years ago, it was surreal and empty. Now it is busier, so we don't go so much. Being in an architectural space helps us t   We like watching people moving through the space. The inspiration used to come from our work spaces, different locations, and unpopulated spaces. We like alternative areas. I don't like to watch other people's work and videos. Ryoko checks out the music videos and stuff, and I see it if she insists I must. Other people may have done a similar thing and I don't want to know that. I want to approach the idea from somewhere else. We like old films: We're really into 1950s and 60s Japanese films, and Jacques Tati films like *Playtime* and *Traffic*. We share a similar taste for this kind of thing."

ne-o are aware that many people found their early work too cold and formalist, obsessed with both the process and techniques of moving image. But just as they morph and displace space, so too have they made efforts to refocus more recent work on their darkly humorous side   n our work now, we have people, stories, and stuff! Humans dig that more, certain things need that," says Knight.

"I think we have a good blend now. My background is in music and graphics. It's a structured thing. Ryoko is into strange literature, manga, and bizarre stories. I don't have that. I read a lot of Haruki Murakami a while ago, which was good for me, because it is coming from somewhere crazy and bizarre. He's good at giving an almost David Lynch-like screenplay feel to his stories. I haven't read many books before."

That love of strangeness presents itself in comedy drawn out through quirky scenarios, as witnessed through their spots for Egg (where scientists are studying diminutive humanoid hamsters), and their *Late at Night* video for Futureshock, which was significant in redressing perceptions in this regard.

"Jacques Tati is really interesting for that: At one and the same time his work can be quite slapstick but very stylized. It is quite staged and unusual, which makes it very odd. *Playtime* is amazingly filmed; futuristic but still grounded in its time."

ne-o display a futurism in their own work through a deadpan style thousands of miles away from the gonzo stunts and informal zaniness many of their contemporaries use in music video. This is perhaps why their preferred filming location is Tokyo. In the Futureshock video, the city's neon glow elicits a bodypopping flow from cops to commuters, construction works and pension-age denizens of the metropolis. This is street culture as virus infecting the city. There is the host and there is the parasite.

So too in the timelapse world of Miho's *Storyboard* video, the beauty of Tokyo comes to the fore in the empty parks and elevated roadways of its night, humanity locked inside the motion trails of lit vehicles streaming through the city arteries. In *The Boxer* video for The Chemical Brothers, a basketball flies at high velocity through parking lot levels, down office corridors, between the street furniture of Budapest with increasing frenzy.

ne-o have moved from being students of the spatio-temporal, to seriocomic mavericks, through pushing qualities of their personal and professional work diligently between each area. It is this quality more than any other that has framed them in a central space among this next-generation of directors. >>>

(01)

(03)

(02)

(04)

■ THE BOXER

► THE CHEMICAL BROTHERS

Promos for The Chemical Brothers are of a consistently high standard, mainly due to the fact that Tom and Ed only ever appear obliquely in their videos. In this case, they flatten the star of the clip—an overactive basketball—with a truck. Some might call it their first action sequence. *The Boxer* could be considered a high-octane version of one of the most famous short films ever made, Albert Lamorisse's Oscar-winning *The Red Balloon*. While that short was a poetic 1956 study of a boy befriended by a balloon, here the action is reversed and revved up, with the basketball defiantly trying to bounce away from a city street kid.

"It was filmed in Budapest over a couple of days. Originally we were on holiday in Hong Kong and had an awful situation, as we were in an active pitch for a famous band and we didn't like the music," says Knight. "We were sent a track which had this awful DRM attached and it was frustrating us trying to play it through dial-up connection. Someone else sent us another track which was a simple mp3. Through all the stress, Ryoko had the idea of a ball connected through things. I didn't quite understand the idea at first, and through a process of miscommunication, we wrote something about a crazy basketball. It is probably the quickest treatment we've ever written.

"The reason for the location stems from the music in the actual video. The ball needs to bounce synchronized with the 16th or 8th beat in the track. To do that, we needed a space with equidistant or closed surfaces to bounce around. A roof low to the floor but with uprights. Obviously parking lots are ideal. So the location thing happened mainly so it would't fly into the sky. Being connoisseurs of parking lots, we wanted to find a good example. But it was a technical reason that made us go with it." >>>

(05)

(06)

(07)

● SLATE

STYLE: FLUID LIVE ACTION WITH VISUAL EFFECTS.
DISTINGUISHING FEATURE: SEAMLESS VIRTUAL
BASKETBALL INTEGRATION INTO LIVE SCENERY
PROCESS: SHOT ON ARRI SUPER 16MM FILM
CAMERA, THEN EDITED IN PREMIERE PRO.
COMPOSITED IN DISCREET INFERNO WITH
3D ANIMATION USING SOFTIMAGE
POST PRODUCTION: THE MILL
VIDEO FOR ALBUM: *PUSH THE BUTTON*,
THE CHEMICAL BROTHERS

(08)

(09)

(10)

II

[01–07] ne-o's characteristic use of graphic
cityscapes and archetypal urban structures is
evident as the camera follows a basketball's
manic attempts to escape the city
[08–10] An early short, *b3*, highlights the
refinement in technique and ideas of
ne-o's work through time, while also
illustrating a continuing obsession
with empty architectural zones

■ LATE AT NIGHT
▶ FUTURESHOCK

A breakthrough video for ne-o, *Late at Night* fuses the duo's dry humor with their unique take on urban street style and architectural cool. Nighttime vignettes are animated in highly graphic slow-moving shots by the nocturnal breakdancing antics of Tokyo city denizens.

"This was excellent fun to film," Knight remembers. "Because summer can be so hot, it's cooler to be up at night filming. We looked all over Tokyo for locations; we had a hard time finding the right convenience store. We spent all week trying to find a good one, and on the last night we found one right by the hotel. It was a brand new Family Mart, there was the one guy, looked about 16, working there on his own, and we went around with our camera on a tripod blatantly taking shots. Normally you'd be totally busted for this, but the guy worked around us, and edged out of our way. We filmed the dancers in London on what seemed like the hottest day of the year. The rushes are hilarious, watching these old people in woolly hats against green screens at the height of summer." >>>

■■

[01–02] Creating 3D composites for the video backgrounds using Combustion
[03–04] Filming green screen elements
[05–18] Bodypopping in Tokyo

● SLATE

STYLE: LIVE ACTION/PHOTOGRAPHIC HYBRID COMPOSITE
DISTINGUISHING FEATURE: BODYPOPPING ACTOR COMPOSITES
PROCESS: USED A ARRI SUPER 16MM FILM CAMERA (DANCERS) & 35MM STILLS CAMERA FOR BACKGROUNDS. EDITED USING PREMIERE PRO WITH COMPOSITING IN DISCREET COMBUSTION / EYEON DIGITAL FUSION
POSTPRODUCTION: EYECANDY LTD
VIDEO FOR ALBUM: *PHANTOM THEORY*, FUTURESHOCK

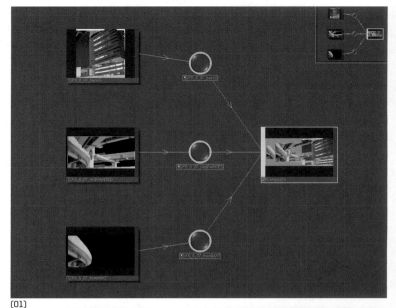

[01]

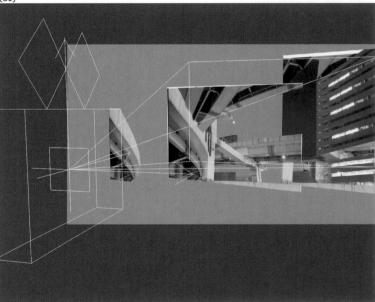

[02]

[03]

[04]

(05)

(06)

(07)

(08)

(09)

(10)

(11)

(12)

(13)

(14)

(15)

(16)

(17)

(18)

(01)

(06)

(02)

(07)

(03)

(08)

(04)

(09)

(05)

(10)

(11)

(12)

■ VISIONARY WORLD
▶ KEN ISHII

Jacques Tati meets Fritz Lang in this modernist mograph concept piece for Japanese DJ Ken Ishii's visual album.

Knight: "This involved getting up early and flying up to a television factory near Newcastle. We wanted to go there to film crazy robots. The best one they had had a white costume on. Amongst these other red robots with its cloth costume, it looked like a stupid raver at a party. In the end we didn't use it though as it looked too organic. What was funny was that some of the robots had dropped the TV tubes. They had shattered glass all around them. The factory was a great place to film. Then we had to laboriously cut them out. Some of the interior shots are Hong Kong B Power Station; we had a very helpful visit there to take some shots. It is a nice power station that recycles dust to make cement."

● SLATE

STYLE: HIGHLY PHOTOGRAPHIC, ABSTRACT
DISTINGUISHING FEATURE: MINIMAL
FLAT GRAPHIC CUT-OUT STYLE
PROCESS: PANASONIC VARICAM HD CAMERA (ROBOTS)
AND MAMIYA 6 CAMERA (BACKGROUNDS AND PLATES),
EDITED USING PREMIERE PRO, WITH COMPOSITING USING
DISCREET COMBUSTION / EYEON DIGITAL FUSION
POSTPRODUCTION: EYECANDY LTD
VIDEO FOR ALBUM: *FUTURE IN LIGHT REMIXED
AND VISUALIZED*, KEN ISHII

❚❚

[01–10] Industrial and cityscape cut-outs create a futuristic environment
[11] Still from *Salaryman 6* short film, refining architectural mutation
[12] Motion trails for Nike's *Art Of Speed* project
[13–16] Tokyo in a state of serenity for *Storyboard*

[13]

■ STORYBOARD
▶ MIHO

ne-o know how to give their environments life. Whereas with some directors, strangely framed and filtered shots become decorative self-indulgence to juice up an artist's vocals, ne-o enhance Japanese songstress Miho's performance through intricate compositing. By doing so, in addition to timelapse tricks, they give the city a delicate pulse.

Knight says, "Making this promo was a nice experience. We went to Tokyo, hanging out at midnight in the summertime, taking timelapse films of everything that moved. We didn't bother to adjust our body clocks, so lived at night. We got into a great vibe with that jetlag thing, living late in the evening." ■

[14]

[15]

● SLATE

STYLE: LIVE ACTION, WITH COMPOSITING
DISTINGUISHING FEATURE: TIMELAPSE
PROCESS: SHOT ON PANASONIC LC1 DIGITAL STILL CAMERA, AND PANASONIC DVX100 DV CAMERA. EDITED USING PREMIERE PRO WITH COMPOSITING IN DISCREET COMBUSTION / EYEON DIGITAL FUSION
POSTPRODUCTION: EYECANDY LTD
VIDEO FOR ALBUM: *MURMUR*, MIHO

[16]

PLEIX

Pleix are a self-described "virtual community of digital artists," made up of a diverse range of seven French audiovisual talents; from the fields of 3D animation, graphic design, and music. I first heard of Pleix's work when they sent me a link for their first clip back in 2001, and promptly included it in the cinema program of motion graphics work I was finalizing. The way they play with abstract ideas then fuse them to pertinent contexts makes them stand out from other stylists. Nowhere is this more so than in their clip for the Kid 606 promo *Sometimes*.

Sometimes is an indirect elegy to 9/11. Subtle use of motion graphics and compositing in this seminal Kid 606 music video release is a textbook illustration of how radical ideas can be woven into the fabric of an essentially promotional form. Previous work for Futureshock and Plaid are more shout-out-effects-driven, but the plaintive tone of *Sometimes*, with its gracefully exploding skyscraper, unhurried editing, and understated angles (witness the shadows of the geometric debris falling past concrete walls) is a fitting motion sculpture and memorial to the World Trade Center disaster. As the virtual shards recombine as the video ends, we are left with an answer to a complex equation of human motivations that offers grace and hope. *Sometimes* offers the answer to people who suggest motion graphics is about technique and style without any emotional or narrative context. It doesn't have to be this way, and the next generation of music video directors knows this.

"For *Sometimes*, we shot hundreds of buildings around Paris and found some on Google," say Pleix as a "collective voice."

"Then we just composited simple CG shapes onto them. The hardest job was to find contrasting frames between each shot. We tried different looks for *Sometimes*. We tested handheld camera moves, but it offered too much realism and killed the poetry and pacing of the piece. The response to this echo of 9/11 was very soft and easy. Maybe we didn't take it far enough?"

Essentially a hybrid of short film and promotional video, Pleix later reapplied the look of *Sometimes*, the fragmented, free-floating glossy blocks—diminutive versions of Kubrick's ominous black onyx obelisk in *2001: A Space Odyssey*—to a commercial spot for Audi. "We didn't have any qualms about reapplying this idea for a commercial; we must eat and pay our rent each month, so making a big-budget commercial based on our artistic work was OK. And if we had refused that script, the agency would have found somebody else to make it, so we were happy to control the whole thing."

" We are returning to more sophisticated images, heavier in terms of post-production. It's a kind of cycle: Simple, then more complex, then back to simple things again" PLEIX

Through their commercial, music video and personal work, Pleix's egalitarian construct of digital artisans aim to highlight the limits, contradictions, and accidents that present the fragility of the digital world.

"Our first pieces were very abstract and more minimal in a sense. Now they are more complex, more photorealistic, and maybe more ambitious," they insist, regarding the evolution of their work. "We made those minimal pieces when we started Pleix, three or four years ago. Before Pleix, we used to do photorealistic CGI in post-production companies, and 3D animation and photoreal integration for other directors on ads or feature films. Pleix acted as a freedom bubble for us. It was the place where we could forget about high-end CG shaders and heavy post-production. So we started naturally with these abstract pieces. Now we are returning to more sophisticated images, heavier in terms of post-production. It's a kind of cycle: Simple, then more complex, then back to simple things again... Like the clothes you wear or the food you have day after day."

Pleix have been at the forefront of the new French digital animation wave that quickly followed and complemented the explosion in the Parisian electronic music scene.

"We try to not to have a 'touch' coming from our technique or the subjects we treat. Because we are seven people, with seven different ways of thinking, it is hard to categorize our work. But we all come from the same place, Paris, and we are all influenced by the same things from our childhoods—video games, TV, and other electronic stuff."

There is no great secret in the way the group process this information to make their moving image work, but it does indicate why they prefer a group dynamic as opposed to acting individually. Can anyone really be alone in their atelier anymore, when there are so many virtual connections to be made?

"We find our inspiration in our society, our world which is full of contradictions. We usually try to have a few readings in our films, a bit like a subliminal message. You can watch our videos without thinking about it, or you might notice it and find something more sensitive. People are free to see what they want. We are not so different from other artists but we've got our tastes, our own desires, our sense of humor. Being seven makes our inspiration sources very large, coming from many different fields—like cinema, art, TV, comic books, and cartoons.

"The main thing is, we like producing tension between graphics, videos, sounds, and edit that generate different ambiences and atmospheres. Work that is on the edge of things. And we all love using technical accidents when they come out nicely! We love being surprised and sharing our work with the public. This is why we use all different fields to show our films: Exhibitions, festivals, and the Internet. Our Web site is simple to read and easy to update and the perfect place to share our last projects. When we finish a film, we put it on the Web right away, we all love the Internet."

This *need* to share sets Pleix apart from previous experimenters in moving image, the video artists and practitioners whose only means of output historically was through specialized and mediated distribution— through galleries, and ivory-towered institutions. The promotional video offers the best chance to get these experiments viewed by the masses.

"Music video doesn't change so much on TV. Now, because of the DVD market, we do more small music videos with smaller budgets but bigger freedom." There are trade-offs to be made, but opportunities within that. Pleix cater to this structure through their range of work that feeds off and complements each other, as opposed to the old-style of video director who aligned his or her vision directly with the artist from one commercial job to the next.

"The industry defines very soon what your style will be and which new hole you will fill. The hardest job to do is the one you would like to avoid. Lots of directors are stuck in a style that fits with the industry but not into their own personality." Something Pleix have made a strategy of avoiding. >>>

[01]

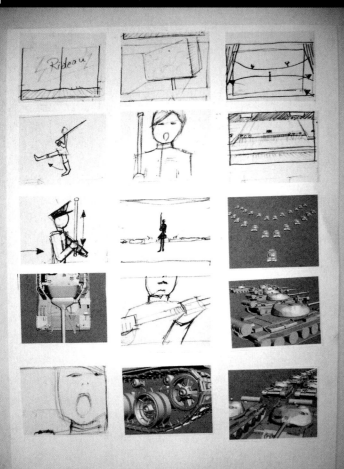

[02]

■ CISH CASH
► BASEMENT JAXX

Cish Cash sees Pleix bringing disco propaganda to life. Siouxsie Sioux is the militaristic majorette orchestrating a post-Red Square parade of virtual military might. The clip is a witty take on the dance choreography of a Busby Berkeley-style musical, with tanks, jets, and choppers substituting for legs, palm frond headdresses, and "spirit fingers."

Pleix: "With all the images of war on TV, we wanted to do a 'ballet' of helicopters, planes, and such, executing some impressive aerial maneuvers. We wanted just one actor: The majorette. It's not propaganda for war but we like using what surrounds us, in our society. Then, the ideas came naturally, watching TV or listening to people talking about it all the time. We focus on the music to find a narrative line and this idea came to us. We were free to do what we wanted and we never met the band. It was very cool to do but a lot of work!" >>>

■■

[01–02] Storyboard notebook scans
[03–13] *Cish Cash* is disco propaganda at its best. Red Square parades were never this much fun

(03)

(08)

(12)

(04)

(09)

(05)

(10)

(06)

(11)

(13)

(07)

● SLATE

STYLE: 3D ANIMATION
DISTINGUISHING FEATURE:
ABSTRACT MILITARY PROPAGANDA PARADE
PROCESS: 3D ANIMATION WITH GREEN SCREEN LIVE ACTION
VIDEO FOR ALBUM: *CISH CASH*, BASEMENT JAXX

Sometimes is an experimental music clip mined for ideas in a follow-up commercial spot for an Audi commercial, which sees the automobile shatter rather than a skyscraper. This astounding promo is a seminal piece and one of the most powerful I've come across in recent years. A high-rise explodes into virtual blocks that float and bounce in slow motion through urban space, eventually attracting each other in a force of will that sees them converge, reconfigured as a whole. It deserves a place in MoMA's permanent collection of moving image for the way it marries the simplicity of its vision to seamless motion graphic technique, creating a spine-tingling, haunting resonance.

"*Sometimes* is, before anything else, a work of dynamic and energetic destruction," say the Pleix collective. "The origin of the project is, of course, the horrible event of 9/11, but it's also the explosion scene of *Zabriskie Point*, the Michelangelo Antonioni film. *Sometimes* is an association of those two visions. We didn't want to make a political point. For this project, Pleix's analysis is simply 'physical;' for out of all destruction comes evolution." >>>

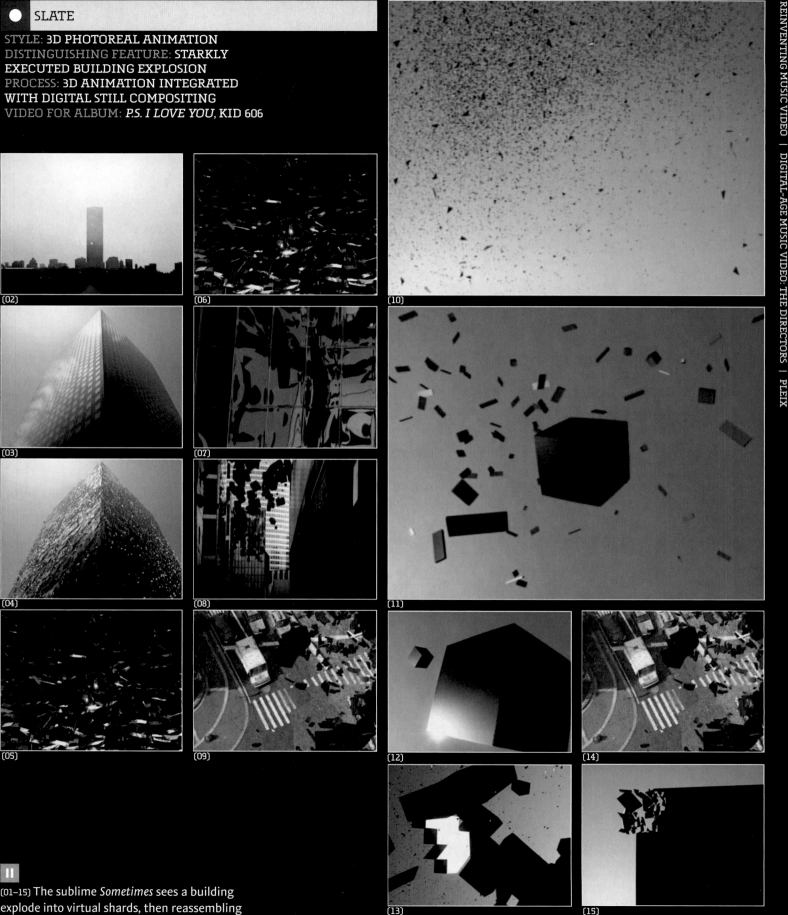

● SLATE

STYLE: **3D PHOTOREAL ANIMATION**
DISTINGUISHING FEATURE: **STARKLY EXECUTED BUILDING EXPLOSION**
PROCESS: **3D ANIMATION INTEGRATED WITH DIGITAL STILL COMPOSITING**
VIDEO FOR ALBUM: *P.S. I LOVE YOU*, KID 606

(02)

(06)

(10)

(03)

(07)

(11)

(04)

(08)

(05)

(09)

(12)

(14)

(01–15) The sublime *Sometimes* sees a building explode into virtual shards, then reassembling

(13)

(15)

BUILDING 437768WVB9

BUILDING 437768WVB9

(02)

■ PRIDE'S PARANOÏA
► FUTURESHOCK

"Shinya Tsukamoto's *Tetsuo: Iron Man* was a source of inspiration for the Futureshock video. And also *Akira* by Katsuhiro Otomo," say Pleix. "Many mangas and a lot of Japanese cyberpunk influences influenced this video and, of course, our old Transformers robot toys!"

A riot of post-apocalyptic, late-capitalist elements fuse in Futureshock's post-humanist, neon-hued, urban adventure. >>>

■■

(01) Concept illustration where Corbusier is funnelled through ultra-contemporary Tokyo-Nagoya-Osaka megalopolis
(02) The Futureshock cityscape and man-machine protagonist is straight out of *Tetsuo: Iron Man*

Adam Levite AKA Associates in Science / Bessy & Combe / Brand New School / Ben Dawkins / Martin de Thurah / Chris Milk / Hideaki Motoki / Muto Musashi / ne-o / Pleix / Jonas Odell / +cruz / Ramon & Pedro / Vernie Yeung / Woof Wan-Bau

(01)

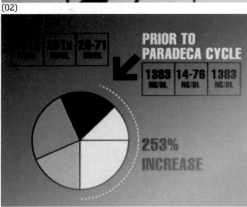

(02)

(03)

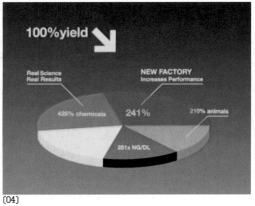

(04)

(05)

(06)

(07)

(08)

ITSU
▶ PLAID

Pork Corp glints as a perfect
abstract of a US corporate HQ.
In a stylized boardroom, animated
spreadsheets, bar graphs, and
pie charts illustrate corporate
greed. Fawning executives grow
pig faces, making clear the base
animalistic instincts on show.
Promotional video as activist art.

(01–08) Pleix create a graphic playground out
of corporate dystopia and infographics

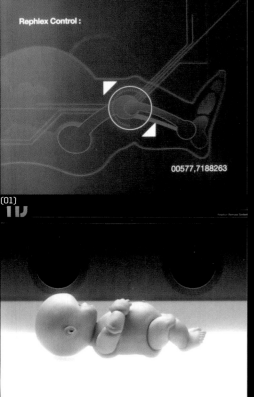

Rephlex Control :

00577,7188263

(01)

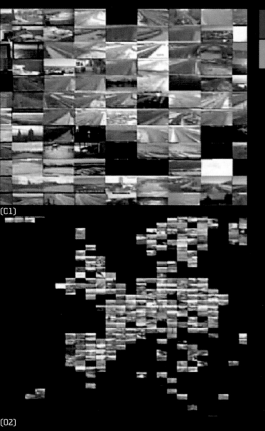

(02)

■ E-BABY
► BLEIP

A mother's interaction with her baby is mediated through technological barriers. *E-Baby* comments on the way technology and machines are interjecting into the world of the natural and biological. While this can be helpful and enhance the environment or outcome of things, it is at other times an unwelcome distraction and intervention in something that should be enjoyed for what it is, without artificiality.

Pleix: "The inspiration was surrealist artist Hans Bellmer's imagined world of *Coppelia*. For a while, we wanted to work on dolls, on an automatons world, and a film about the relation of distance. The kind of relation we all have now, speaking with each other, not face to face, but via phone, mail, and text. Is it possible to have real feelings with distance? The fusion of those desires generated the *E-Baby* project. The idea came before the music. Thanks to a great collaboration with Bleip [the Pleix collective's musician], showing him the images as a work in progress, he succeeded in creating the right music for the atmosphere of the short."

II

(01–02) A statement on artificiality
and technological interference

■ NETLAG
► BLEIP

Infographics and communication made visible is a recurring Pleix motif. *Netlag* uses webcam and random broadcasts to show the activities and intricacies of the world through panning and scanning, floating in and zooming out of information flows and geographic locations from a top-down view of the world. It's a beautiful exercise but ultimately feels like a test for a telecommunications company commercial. >>>

II

(01–02) Beautiful infographics

(C1)

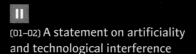

(02)

(01)

(02)

Pleix go all "chara chara" (something that is too flashy in terms of style) in this neon-graduated photomontage. This clip remakes Terry Gilliam's *Monty Python* animations through the lens of Japanese teen girls—it is all Barbie doll legs, plush soft dolls, flouro colors, and eye-catching shapes without context. Only the power drill dildo stuck between the legs of a girl and a male model body suggests a note of humorous dissent. This is either a joke being played on the viewer, or simply graphic eye candy. ■

II

(01–02) A virtual reimaging of the game, *Simon*
(03–05) Graphic photomontage

■ SIMONE
▶ BLEIP

A high-concept performance piece, *Simone* is a simple short focusing on a color box that traps a girl within a virtual code game. Performance art for a post-MTV generation.

Pleix: "The *Simone* concept was to create a simple rule like 'I do some tricks, you must do the same.' This is the Milton Bradley *Simon* game concept: Some of us spent hours playing this game, feeling like they were playing with someone living far from the earth. It also could have been a language. We are also crazy about the Ridley Scott opening for *Alien*, the look and the sound design of the SOS. We don't understand anything but it sounds like a conversation with questions and answers. Of course we also had in mind Spielberg's *Close Encounters of the Third Kind*. We did the first edit of the film without any sounds and Bleip [Pleix's musician] made the sound following the 'rule:' One color for each tone. This also equated to what *Simone* looks like."

[03]

[04]

[05]

JONAS ODELL

Jonas Odell's work is like a motion sketchbook, his ideas fly off the page and straight onto the screen. It's like his mind prints them to video without going through the process other directors might of configuring them into living things or real-world objects. In this Swedish director's best-known works—the *Take Me Out* music video for Franz Ferdinand, or Goldfrapp's *Strict Machine*—the music clip plays like a motion canvas. A Pop Art screenprint come to life.

"I just feel that printed graphics are usually more inspiring than animation, I guess," says Odell. He makes obvious reference to this in most of his music videos, but even in commercial spots, such as for BMW Series 1, the screen is littered with crop marks and CMYK print markers.

"Insofar that there is a particular style, I think it comes from me using various mixed techniques to get the result I want. To me, it isn't so much a style as an approach, though, and I hope that each project has its own distinctive look."

Odell's motion graphics are still attached to the printed page. They haven't quite broken free from their frozen graphic past. This works particularly well when the band also have a graphic sensibility—this is why Odell and Franz Ferdinand gelled so well.

"It's really about treating the film as a whole, rather than a linear approach of finishing off scene after scene. It's all about working like a sculptor, chiselling away and shaping the film, looking at it from all angles and points in time, until you have the film you want" JONAS ODELL

"The band themselves had the idea that t̶h̶e̶y̶ ̶w̶a̶nted something in the Dada style, b̶e̶i̶n̶g̶ a fan of that movement, I̶ ̶n̶a̶t̶u̶r̶ally jumped on the assignment. I was already familiar with a lot of Dada art, so we could create artwork in that style, but I also wanted to connect the visuals to the music. 'Post punk' is probably a description that the band doesn't want to hear, but the music draws on influences from the late 1970s/early 1980s, a time and genre of music where record covers were often influenced by Dada and other related art movements. So, I wanted the Dada influences to be filtered through this punk and post-punk approach as well."

And Goldfrapp, where he really found his voice? "In the case of Goldfrapp's *Stric̶t̶ Machine*, I thought I heard echoes of various styles of music in the track: electronica, disco, and even a hint of glam rock, and I wanted to include various visual elements reflecting these styles; so I thought a collage format would help bring everything together. I also felt there was kind of a hypnotic feel to the track that I wanted to represent using kaleidoscopic and symmetric imagery. Looking at their previous videos, I also decided to focus more on the singer than had been done previously, so I placed her in the middle of all these symmetric graphics that seemed to point to the center of the frame.

"As for the work process, it's really about treating the film as a whole, rather than a linear approach of finishing off scene after scene. It's all about working like a sculptor, chiselling away and shaping the film, looking at it from all angles and points in time, until you have the film you want. No part is complete until the whole is finished."

Odell's directorial style doesn't veer between techniques; there is a limited play in his range that he appears happy to hone and perfect. What does he feel about his range of references, particularly to the art world?

"I have not really explored it myself, I think it probably comes from an interest in art—and maybe from overdosing on art books during the period when most of the music videos I've made have been produced. Obviously the industry has the power to choose which direction music videos are going; if the record label doesn't like your style, you don't get to make videos. Apart from that, I really think the background defines your style, what ideas pop up in your head as you hear a piece of music." >>>

[01]

■ TAKE ME OUT
► FRANZ FERDINAND

An art school student notepad, animated. The band's association with Russian avant-garde imagery is applied to the video with Alexander Rodchenko-style squares scrolling past in black, red, and white blocks. Dadaist imagery mixes with woodcut illustrations, medical diagrams, and cartography. Jonas Odell takes a mental snapshot of the band's Glasgow School of Art origins, and applies it faithfully and fluidly in a motion graphics melée. >>>

[02]

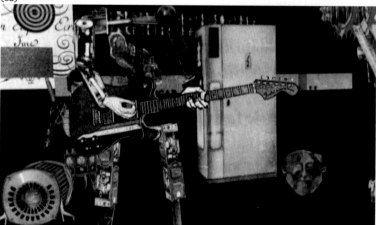

[03]

■

(01–10) The bands art school origins are reflected by the video's influences

(04)

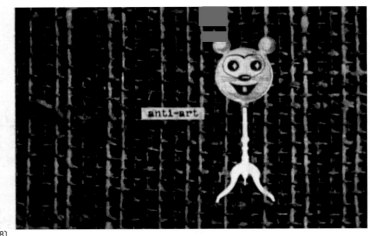

(08)

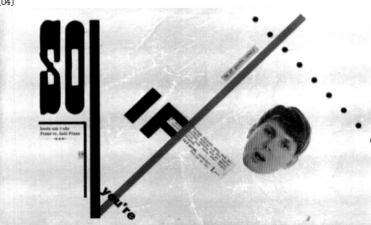

(05)

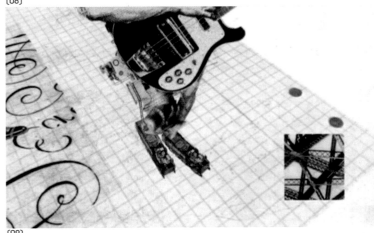

(09)

(06)

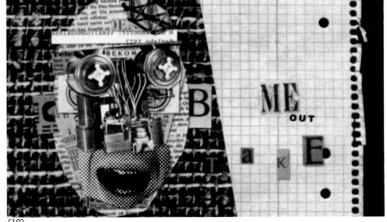

(10)

(07)

● SLATE

STYLE: **ANIMATION/LIVE ACTION HYBRID**
DISTINGUISHING FEATURE: **DADAIST PRINT STYLINGS**
PROCESS: **FILMED PERFORMANCE AGAINST GREEN SCREEN. ANIMATION AND COMPOSITING**
VIDEO FOR ALBUM: ***FRANZ FERDINAND*, FRANZ FERDINAND**

(01)

(05)

(02)

(06)

(03)

(07)

(04)

(08)

(09)

(10)

(11)

■ FEELING A MOMENT
▶ FEEDER

Grant Nicholas, lead singer of Feeder, is isolated from a street scene, with a protective graphic zone of flat blocks wiping out a layer of texture—the layer of reality—around him. A departure from Odell's other work, it feels like the band are caught in a hyperreal computer game level, where their seemingly naturalistic street scene setting is a virtual 3D model. With blocks showing deliberately bad collision detection, and the photoreal textures being washed away to white, the director elevates a performance video to a meditation on artificial reality.

■

(01–11) East End in *The Matrix*. Artifice and reality collide, Odell-style

[01]

[03]

[04]

[05]

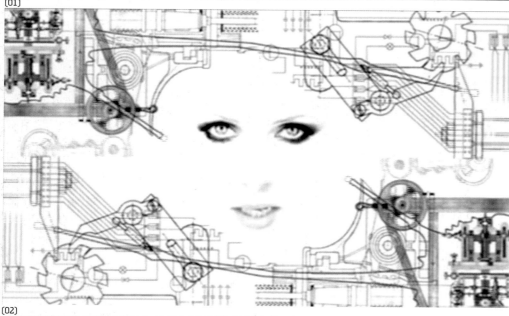

[02]

[06]

■ STRICT MACHINE
▶ GOLDFRAPP

Goldfrapp's sonic oscillations are duplicated on screen in this graphic ode to glam. Body parts are isolated and repeated in an abstracted kaleidoscopic array, while wolf-headed businessmen prowl the screen watching the undulating figure of Alison Goldfrapp's Little Red Riding Hood, all grown-up.

● SLATE

STYLE: ANIMATION/LIVE ACTION HYBRID
DISTINGUISHING FEATURE: LAYERED, MIRRORED, AND DUPLICATED GEOMETRIC IMAGERY
PROCESS: FILMED PERFORMANCE AGAINST GREEN SCREEN. ANIMATION AND COMPOSITING
VIDEO FOR ALBUM: *BLACK CHERRY*, GOLDFRAPP

(01–06) The glamorous graphic style captures the look and feel of the band and their sound

(01–02)

SHOT YOU DOWN

AUDIOBULLYS

Audiobullys demands a harsher graphic treatment, harking to a post-punk print esthetic more in tune with their harder sound.

(03–06)

SMILE

MAD ACTION

Odell further polishes his trademark style, showboating through a history of modern art. A hand-drawn motion illustrative head shot of the singer soon develops into more recognizable art world styles. Pencil jottings turn into line drawings then Magritte, Braque, Picasso—we realize we are going through a random history of modern art here—Gilbert and George, Pop Art, Punk, Antonio Tapies, Barbara Kruger, then back to Mucha, and snapping to evocations of Nam June Paik's video art. The ink drips off the vocalist's face, leaving a blank canvas. We are left with a flurry of references and a satisfying hit of art history. Thoroughly educational.

(07–08)

CHANGES

TAHITI 80

A simple stop-motion odyssey of rotating buildings, and indoor/outdoor furnished temporality. Cod surrealist eye candy. ◾

(01)

(02)

(03)

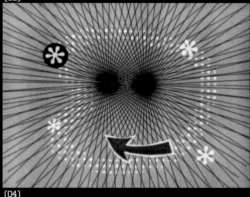

(04)

(05)

(06)

(07)

(08)

VIDEOGRAPHY

WAMONO,	HIFANA
AKERO,	HIFANA
NU WORLD,	LEYONA
DIGITAL BREATH,	AFRA
MISERARETE,	JUDY ONGG
FAT BROS,	HIFANA
THE ATTACK OF THE NINJA,	DJ UPPERCUT
EXIT/DELETE_FIRST_SIGHT,	TAKAGI MASAKATSU

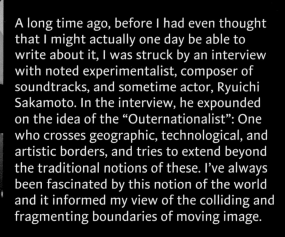

A long time ago, before I had even thought that I might actually one day be able to write about it, I was struck by an interview with noted experimentalist, composer of soundtracks, and sometime actor, Ryuichi Sakamoto. In the interview, he expounded on the idea of the "Outernationalist": One who crosses geographic, technological, and artistic borders, and tries to extend beyond the traditional notions of these. I've always been fascinated by this notion of the world and it informed my view of the colliding and fragmenting boundaries of moving image.

The loudest echoes of this Outernationalist philosophy I've located are in the work of +cruz, noted art director for the advertising agency Wieden+Kennedy's Tokyo Lab, the agency's record label spin-off. Here, +cruz has been in an admirable position to push his take on the quintessential Tokyo hybrid style, as an outsider and foreigner within a culture which is dichotomously insular with an insatiable desire for the exotic (or foreign). A self-styled "Flipachinko"—an attempt to conflate his diverse Filipino, Chinese, and Spanish heritage—this director has orchestrated moving images that resonate with a global, Asian, and individual style. "I'm kind of a hybrid anomaly," he tells me. "You cannot really be one thing these days."

With a background in illustration and graphic design, +cruz has worked previously with Wieden+Kennedy Portland, Imaginary Forces, Razorfish London, Oceanmonsters, and Motion Theory, before finding a home at Wieden+Kennedy Tokyo. He credits a three-and-a-half month exploration of Asia where he was "mesmerized by its dynamic beauty and chaos," for his desire to settle in that environment. The proximity to China and its reawakening and transition from a "counterfeit culture" to creative powerhouse makes Asia somehow more relevant for him as a creative base.

"I was born and raised in the Philippines until I was 13, when I emigrated to the US. I lived and worked in both the US and Europe for the first six years of my career, and realized that so much of the world is defined by Western schools of thought, visually speaking, because schools and universities teach with Western methods of thinking and design. Even if you look at the Web, most of this virtual space is homogenous, based on a predominantly American look. Whoever controls media, controls the world. I want to change that by helping to elevate Asian consciousness globally through art and design.

REINVENTING MUSIC VIDEO | DIGITAL-AGE MUSIC VIDEO: THE DIRECTORS | +CRUZ

"There is no quicker or more critical and discerning eye than the Japanese youth, so you have to stay ahead of the curve" +cruz

"Every time I release work, I am quite conscious about representing an Asian esthetic in the global broadcast. I feel pride in representing my peeps globally. It's important to cultivate Asia as a creative powerhouse, not just be big in Japan, not just copying the US or Europe. We need to unite as a culture and help impact the world around us, show our history and tradition and stop being known as a 'counterfeit culture.' The ultimate goal is to reverse colonialization. I would love to see the day when Asia is the main superpower; or at least global equilibrium. Hopefully in this lifetime."

+cruz's interest in going beyond the counterfeit and creating with originality is a particular flashpoint at the moment. There has been rising debate about the idea of *pakuri* within Japanese art. Roughly translated, the verb's meaning is "to rip off or steal an idea," and has been refined by Tokyo ex-pat, David Marx, as: "An artistic use of creative elements from other works, used within a similar context without acknowledgement of the original." This has been fairly common within a Japanese culture that is used to the old and new co-existing together, with contexts and ideas free-floating in an unselfconscious way.

+cruz sees this collision between the traditional and futuristic as part of Japan's soul. Latterly, this freeform creativity has been one of the West's main draws to Japan as a creative center, particularly as the country has more recently become confident in drawing upon itself for this energy rather than borrowing from overseas.

+cruz is particularly interesting as a director and creative producer because he has thought through a philosophy he labels, "Asia nowhere: now here." It is a philosophy and stance that gives his work more meaning than a particular style or artist can possibly bring on its own, and offers a route beyond *pakuri*, and the imitation of other cultural scenes. It is part of a larger manifesto and creative campaign which gives his process and his inspirations more social—even more political—intent. It is a rare and risky strategy.

"I think the work I do stands out because it is different from everything else out there. It has an unusual hybrid approach and Asian character to it. Even if you compare it to the LA or NYC motion graphics scenes, it looks, feels, and moves differently. It's not as sophisticated with movement, but actually more restrained, and relies more on story and unique character design. There is no quicker or more critical and discerning eye than the Japanese youth, so you have to stay ahead of the curve."

Wieden+Kennedy Tokyo Lab was launched by Wieden+Kennedy's global creative director, John C. Jay, as a basis to go beyond a traditional notion of an agency, to create more of a dialog with mainstream and creative culture, and have active participation within it.

+cruz heads up the visual side of the creative label with a core team of Woog, from Hong Kong, and Shane Lester, from LA. The Lab's output concentrates on integrated audio and visual experiences, and so far comprises the release of two Hifana CD/DVD albums, and other albums by DJ Uppercut, Afra, and Takagi Masakatsu. The label brings in creative teams from globally disparate locations, including, to date: Strange Attractors (The Hague), Kamikaze Douga (Tokyo), Ocean Monsters (LA), and VKR (Seoul).

As their own publishers and creative network, Wieden+Kennedy Tokyo Lab has allowed +cruz an amazing amount of creative freedom and opportunity to produce a wild range of experimental music video output within a short space of time. "Truth is," he confesses, "I started directing because I could not afford to hire real directors.

"Back in the 1980s, when music videos first surfaced, bands took greater risks. The videos were more sensational. I feel as if we are in a state of transition right now. But it's still an exciting time for pop promos because many voices are surfacing and the new generation of musicians are actually directing and making their own videos, which creates a kind of personal indie-broadcast movement." >>>

Adam Levite AKA Associates in Science / Bessy & Combe / Brand New School / Ben Dawkins / Martin de Thurah / Chris Milk / Hideaki Motoki / Muto Musashi / ne-o / Pleix / Jonas Odell / Ramon & Pedro / Vernie Yeung / Woof Wan-Bau

+cruz

HIFANA : WAMONO
STYLE FRAMES
03.09.2005

[01]

■ WAMONO

▶ HIFANA

Wamono means "things Japanese." This animated video for Hifana tries to exemplify this through using ancient Japanese folklore as a jumping-off point to tell the tale of two fishermen—alter egos of the Hifana duo, Juicy and Kiezo—hoping to catch a big Tairyo fish. With its references to seminal 19th-century landscape painter Katsushika Hokusai and other traditional Japanese elements, *Wamono* has a depth and emotional breadth while also managing that difficult feat of being light and breezy, funny, and constantly entertaining.

"We researched Japanisms in-depth," reveals +cruz. "This cinematography is actually inspired by the great Japanese film legend, *Yasujiro Ozu*, with its low, locked-off camera. With respect to authentic Nippon taste, we exercised a lot of restraint, making a specific decision to avoid slick animation moves, usually found in motion graphics. Therefore, all the weight of the video was based on the characters' and supporting characters' movement, acting and emotions, set designs, and, most of all, the story.

"We did two consecutive shoots back-to-back to save money on crew and lights, so we gunned through 30 hours of shooting. *Wamono* was our most ambitious project to date. We produced that video 75 percent in-house, from concept, scripting, storyboards, animatics, editorial, design, character design, set design, animation boards, all the way to final 2D animation and compositing. Definitely the most strenuous video I have ever worked on. It was a small team of four people at W+KTLAB and a team of eight 3D animators from Kamikaze Douga. We purposefully made the motion anti-motion graphics."

■ ■

[01] Style frames and mood board for *Wamano* video
[02] One-sheet visual video treatment
[03–06] Character designs and illustrations of the giant fish, Ebisu, and [overleaf] stills from *Wamono*

(02)

(03)

(04)

(05)

(06)

"Initially, Juicy and Kiezo of Hifana came to us with an idea: 'Two fishermen go out to sea to eat raw fish and somehow we show Okinawa Sanshin [indigenous ethnic guitars] players.'"

The idea of Hifana surfing on a mythical fish came about, and +cruz later discovered the god of fishermen was called Ebisu, and is personified as a giant fish. Using this fictitious fable as a backbone, the team wove the fishermen story alongside a beer commercial that the two fishermen are watching on TV. A weather report foreshadows the dilemma of man against the forces of nature, a storm-fish wave.

"I naturally equated this to the Hokusai's iconic waves. We developed rough designs and style frames and presented the story to Hifana," +cruz explains.

Stick figure storyboards were used as an efficient way to visualize and outline the idea, and these were then cut as an animatic. Kamikaze Douga (formerly of Studio 4° Celsius) were engaged as a 3D animation partner. >>>

● SLATE

STYLE: ANTI-MOTION GRAPHICS
ANIMATED FABLE
DISTINGUISHING FEATURE:
MULTILAYERED ANIMATION STYLES
PROCESS: PANASONIC DVX-100 FOR LIVE
ACTION. 3D MODELLING & ANIMATION, 2D
ANIMATION AND COMPOSITING USING
AFTER EFFECTS AND FINAL CUT PRO
VIDEO FOR ALBUM: *CHANNEL H*, HIFANA

■ DIGITAL BREATH
▶ AFRA

Digital Breath has a unique take on the performance video, foregrounding Afra's human beatbox credentials by making the treatment of his breath the obvious focus of the music video. +cruz and his team sculpt motion visuals around the live action film of the artist to vivid effect.

The director explains: "Afra wanted something organic and real—a sunrise and natural things. John C. Jay and I concepted the video to reinforce the humanity behind the sound. I referenced Charles and Ray Eames' *The Powers of Ten* structurally. At this point, most of our videos were animation-based, but we wanted to capture Afra in as real a way as we could—on film. We also needed to shoot plates of natural landscapes to make a hyperreal Shangri-La composite. Japan proved to be expensive, so we had to think of more cost-effective locations."

The project relocated six people—three from Tokyo and three from LA—to Bangkok for 32 days to produce the video. Wieden+Kennedy Tokyo Lab and Ocean Monsters acted as co-production companies, with local Thai production companies, Triton Films and Finito. "We were like a traveling creative circus act," enthuses +cruz. >>>

(01)

(02)

(03)

▮▮

(01–05) Organic realization of Afra's human beatbox sound
(06) Original treatment

Adam Levite AKA Associates in Science / Bessy & Combe / Brand New School / Ben Dawkins / Martin de Thurah / Chris Milk / Hideaki Motoki / Muto Musashi / ne-o / Pleix / Jonas Odell / Ramon & Pedro / Vernie Yeung / Woof Wan-Bau +cruz

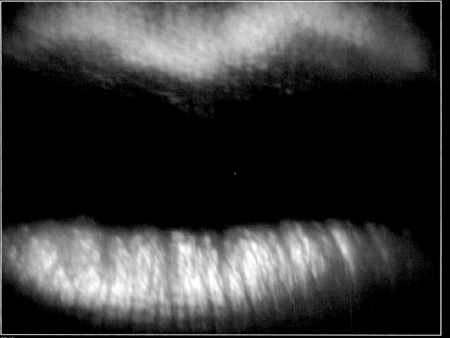
(04)

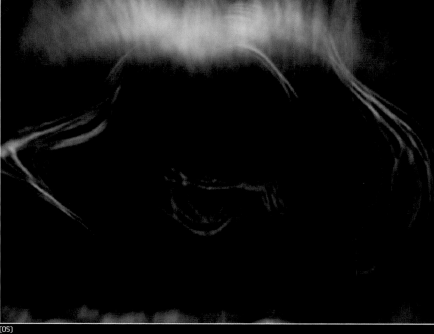
(05)

AFRA: *DIGITAL BREATH* TREATMENT
IDEA.01: ENCHANTED FOREST

Afra beatboxes through an enchanted forest. His digital breath triggers an organic chain reaction as flora and foliage animate in reaction to his urban sounds. At the end of the forest, he arrives at nirvana, a natural Shangri-La revealed by sunrise. The video offers a fresh contrast between Afra's urban rhythm and presence set against a fantastic natural environment.

Like The Powers of Ten, it begins with the universe from inside Afra's mouth.

We open on tight close-up shots of Afra's face, mouth, and hands, abstract details of Afra beatboxing, inhaling, and exhaling, emphasizing his polyrhythmic sense. Camera pulses back and forth reacting to sounds from his mouth.

The dark of night comes alive as natural things grow and respond to Afra's rhythm. We travel from an abstract macrocosmos of flora and fauna to mounds of foliage and earth building, expanding into an enchanted forest. Like a conductor playing a symphonic orchestra, the forest responds musically to Afra's sound pulsations. Birds fly, wild leaves grow in mid air, across a dynamically mutating atmosphere. Life unfolds in a chain reaction triggered by his digital breath.

As the song builds into a subtle climax (keyboards), Afra reaches the edge of the forest, arriving at a cliff to greet the sunrise, shedding warm light, darkness awakens to greet the vivid morning light. Camera pans 180° to arrive at a waterfall (liquid sounds cut to his music).

Music switches gear as the power shuts down, the creation goes in a reverse The Powers of Ten back to the beginning… Camera dive zooms back into Afra's mouth, into his throat; the mechanism that powers his organic breath as it slows down.

 SLATE

STYLE: **LIVE ACTION/ANIMATION COMPOSITE**
DISTINGUISHING FEATURE: **CONTOURING BREATH/ SOUND ANIMATIONS ONTO LIVE ACTION**
PROCESS: **PANASONIC DVX-100 FOR LIVE ACTION. 3D MODELLING & ANIMATION, 2D ANIMATION AND COMPOSITING USING AFTER EFFECTS AND FINAL CUT PRO**
VIDEO FOR ALBUM: ***DIGITAL BREATH*, AFRA**

(01)

(02)

(03)

(01–06) Graffiti and graphic smears
embellish exuberant performances

■ AKERO
► HIFANA

Akero urges you to "open up" to new experiences. The track has an anthemic nature and feel-good factor. With a more free-form use of street cultural style, it is akin to the more scattershot approaches of much of Japanese music video. But as part of the looser aspects of Hifana's *Channel H* DVD visual album, it has its part to play in the whole.

"*Akero* is Hifana's version of a summer song, so it was all about beach, sun, fun, and chicks," explains +cruz. "It was our first hip-hop video complete with bikini-clad Hifana beach gals, so again, having a challenging budget, I collaborated with my motion graphics students at Temple University, Tyler School of Arts, Philadelphia, where I taught. This is an example of a non-existent job because we did not have to do a video for this, but Hifana wanted to, so we obliged and crafted an economical solution, shooting everything in DV, with intent to make it high-contrast black and white.

"We shot, produced, directed, and did all editorial and post work in-house. We experimented with a digital stills camera, as a secondary motion camera, to get high-res sequential stills, and mixed that with live action. Our props consisted of masks of different Hifana characters. This was probably the loosest project we have ever done. We looked at a lot of Picasso paintings. Typically, we have nothing except ideas. We just experiment to see how we can realize these ideas into actualities." >>>

● SLATE

STYLE: ABSTRACT GRAPHICS/
PERFORMANCE HYBRID
DISTINGUISHING FEATURE: NAIVE,
GRAFFITI-STYLE MOTION GRAPHIC
PROCESS: GREEN SCREEN LIVE ACTION
SHOT ON DV WITH DIGITAL STILLS,
COMPOSITED IN AFTER EFFECTS
VIDEO FOR ALBUM: *CHANNEL H*, HIFANA

(04)

(05)

(06)

Adam Levite AKA Associates in Science / Bessy & Combe / Brand New School / Ben Dawkins / Martin de Thurah / Chris Milk / Hideaki Motoki / Muto Musashi / ne-o / Pleix / Jonas Odell / +cruz / Ramon & Pedro / Vernie Yeung / Woof Wan-Bau

■ FAT BROS
▶ HIFANA

Team +cruz present Hifanaland, a graphic-laden, beats-generated illustrated kingdom of an evil tri-mohawked god. Personifications of the Hifana duo do battle in a skateboard-inspired animated world.

+cruz says of the video: "This is probably the most seminal video I have ever worked on, the one that really solidified our label. After doing DJ Uppercut with Ocean Monsters, we went for round two. This time around, we had one and a half months to craft the project. So we began in the same vein, conceptualizing the story based on Hifana's request of making it authentic to skate culture, but having it be something skaters have not seen before in skate graphics.

"Juicy, of Hifana, is a graphic designer who has been creating the Pop Hifana characters for the band, and his brother, Maharo, is an illustrator who drew the dark side of Hifana. So I put 1+1+1=3. Good Hifana vs. Bad Hifana + Skate. So the story created itself once more. All Hifana wanted was precise beat and visual synchronization to emphasize the concept and title of the album, *Fresh Push Breakin,'* and the idea of 'touchable sound.'" >>>

(01)

● SLATE

STYLE: ABSTRACT GRAPHICS
DISTINGUISHING FEATURE: CRUDE
ANIMÉ-FILTERED STYLING
PROCESS: ILLUSTRATIONS
SIMPLY ANIMATED
VIDEO FOR ALBUM: *FRESH
PUSH BREAKIN'*, HIFANA

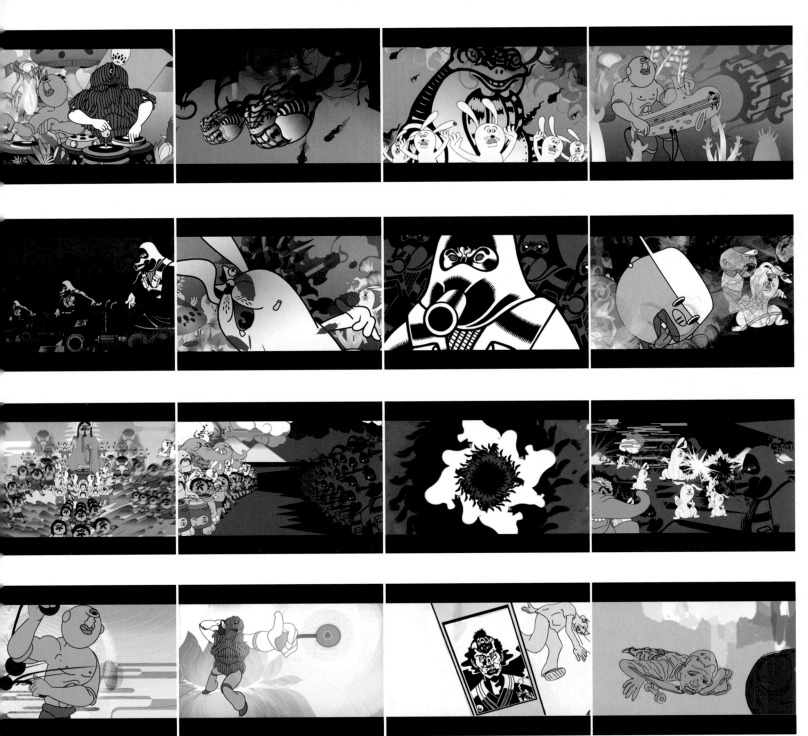

▌▌

[01] *Fat Bros* storyboard

▌▌

Overleaf
[01] *exit/delete_first_site* storyboard
[02–07] Video images animating watercolors and sketches

(01)

■ EXIT/DELETE_FIRST_SIGHT
▶ TAKAGI MASAKATSU

A more abstract, introspective video from +cruz, co-directed with Sun An. With its exploration of more textural, dreamlike forms, the video gives an idea to +cruz's potential range. The Hifana work shows his expertise with animated character and motion graphics. This video is a more poetic and introspective journey that the director describes as: "A daydream in the clouds... impressions that draw from a feeling, a movement, a smile, bygone moments and fading, lost memories.

"Takagi Masakatsu is the epitome of a hybrid musician/artist, creating his own music and videos. He's part of a new breed of post-1980s talent who grew up with technology and uses it fearlessly. This is probably the only music video that Takagi did not do himself. I curated a group show in LA, *ASIA_NO.W.HERE*, featuring Asian artists including myself and Takagi. He gave me a demo copy of his new CD and I kept looping this track on which he was collaborating with David Sylvian. I was extremely infatuated with this Japanese woman in LA at the time and could not get her and that track out of my head, so Takagi had me deal with my feelings by commissioning me to make a video about it. This video was literally a love song. Some people go to therapists, I try to deal with my emotions through my work.

"In one of our conversations, Takagi stated that it is easy to make dark things and have people like it. It's easier for people to relate to. It is much harder to do positive things and have people listen, understand, and like it. That was my challenge. I was always afraid that the video was on the verge of being a maxi-pad tampon commercial!" ■

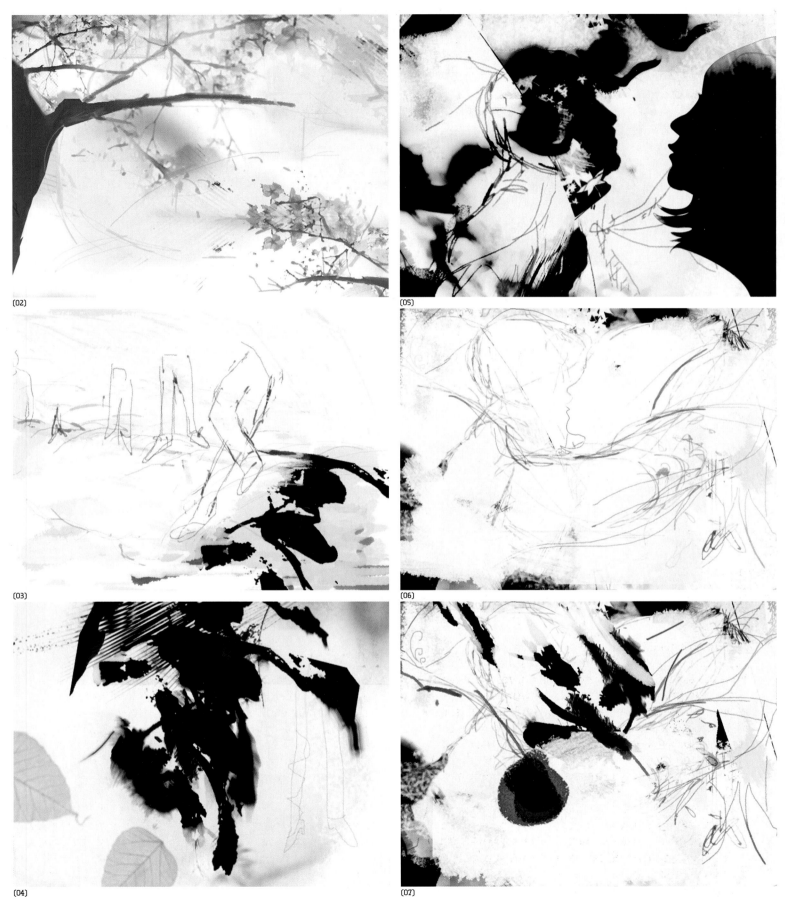

(02)

(05)

(03)

(06)

(04)

(07)

RAMON & PEDRO

Ramon & Pedro cut and splice ideas together in irreverent fashion. Their under-the-radar *The Grey Video*, a moving image accompaniment to the DJ Dangermouse project which reengineered Jay-Z's *The Black Album* wholly from samples taken from The Beatles' *The White Album*, is their signature project so far.

They have also remixed—or at least appropriated—video game culture with a nod to the most addictive game of all time, *Tetris*, in Grand National's *Drink to Moving On*. Actors fill the familiar-colored block costumes in a live-action music clip to amusing effect. More recently, a Sage Francis video has a grittier televisual edge, playing like a 1970s low-budget cop show, but sampling contemporary street culture through a chase of a street-skating icon—the universal icon for a man has come to life, and is being pursued by Francis. The directing team are at their best when the abstract and real meet in lo-fi mashes and clashes.

Ramon & Pedro was born in 2003. Conceived by two Swiss-born, New York-based, classically-trained graphic designers, alumni of celebrated US motion graphics companies, the pseudonymous Ramon & Pedro created a space for the duo to escape from their illustrative roots and move into a more film-focused environment. While they have already created commercial spots for bluechip clients such as VISA, AOL, and VW, they really come into their own executing wry concepts and playful ideas. You can see how this comes through when I ask what first sparked the idea of wanting to get into music video for them. "Moon walking in front of Bob Giraldi's *Beat It*," is the answer. You can see the smirk.

The waggery that everyone got was their video accompaniment to DJ Dangermouse's bootleg homage to The Beatles & Jay-Z. *The Grey Album* begat *The Grey Video*, and its popularity mirrored that of the outrageously successful illicit album. At its height, the video site received 600,000 hits in three days. This would have been more, but the hosting service closed the site down before it sucked up any further bandwidth. The most high-profile example so far of the nascent video mash-up artform, it is a style which can transform the ridiculous into the sublime. These are montages of the wildly incongruous, where the challenge is to find some kind of balance, often between two wildly different artists or styles of music and visuals.

"*The Grey Video* was a spec project that we decided we would do at least a couple of on a yearly basis. We dug the Dangermouse album mostly for its originality. A mash-up of two genres so opposite is a great concept to start with. Of course it does not hurt that both The Beatles and Jay-Z were part of the mix. The idea for the video could not be more basic. We were listening to the album and said if Dangermouse is mixing audio from *The White Album* and *The Black Album*, why don't we create a video where we do the same mash-up, only with imagery?"

The duo explain the process for this defining piece of Internet video history: "The original storyline was to use a performance piece of The Beatles that would slowly but surely be taken over by Jay-Z and urban influences. The first step was to find the right Beatles footage. We settled for *A Hard Day's Night*, which is a little off as far as the era but presented by far the most opportunities for visual effects. There are numerous scenes toward the end where The Beatles perform on stage in front of a crazed teenage audience. The one scene we picked then naturally brought ideas which drove the video. We realized Ringo's drumming podium would make a great DJ booth. At the end of the movie, there's a scene where an old man pops up from a secret trap underneath the stage. That gave us the idea of getting rid of Paul and George to be replaced by the two back-up dancers. The third party—the hyper-nervous show editor—was already playing that role in the flick. The monitors in front of him became a great vehicle to showcase Jay-Z.

"Those moments served to build the skeleton of the video. Then we studied the camera angles to create a rough storyboard and a shot list of what would be recorded later. We had a small studio for half a day and shot everything on Mini-DV against green screen. From there, we researched Jay-Z performance footage. The rest is a lot of editing, and After Effects compositing."

"Storytelling is what captivates us. If, at the end of the day, we can go home having told a great story in a smart and simple fashion, we are happy" RAMON & PEDRO

Although Ramon & Pedro have completed other promos, as well as commissioned short films, these have veered toward more exercises in style or exploration of a particular technique. These are often very well executed, but it is with the dash of the bizarre or farcical when their clips really come to life. "We like Grand National," they say about their first promo, "because we took something everybody relates to and brought it to the next level, which is also true for *The Grey Video* and the Sage Francis promo. It's like revamping the vernacular."

Ramon & Pedro are not arch-stylists or trying to be astounding technical virtuosos, but as they say themselves, "The music itself is often the voice to the directing style." And this, in a nutshell, is how they work: Simply, without pomposity.

"We always try to create something different from our previous pieces. The idea is obviously the most important factor. Our inspiration comes from our past and present. From 'everyday experiences.' We try very hard not to look at other industry work out there. We don't have a style. We always do try to include storytelling and a kiss of humor. We will stop doing music videos the day we can't find a fresh idea." >>>

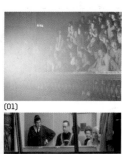
(01)

(06)

(11)

(02)

(07)

(12)

(03)

(08)

(13)

(04)

(09)

(14)

(16)

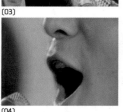
(05)

(10)

(15)

THE GREY VIDEO

▶ DJ DANGERMOUSE AND JAY-2

This famous US TV appearance by The Beatles is hijacked by Ramon & Pedro, who combine archive footage with newly shot elements intended for compositing, and performance footage of Jay-2. This results in the illusion of Ringo on decks not drums, and Lennon breakdancing along to Jay-2's *Encore*. >>>

● SLATE

STYLE: LIVE ACTION/ARCHIVAL FOOTAGE COMPOSITE
DISTINGUISHING FEATURE: POP CULTURAL VIDEO MASH-UP
PROCESS: DV CAMERA STUDIO SHOOT AGAINST GREEN
SCREEN, WITH AFTER EFFECTS, COMPOSITING, AND EDITING
VIDEO FOR ALBUM: N/A

SHOT 1_TAKING OFF THE GUITAR

BACKGROUND

REFERENCE

ACTION

OPTIONAL

close up of JOSH from behind taking off his guitar

close up of JOSH from behind taking off his guitar helped by one of the girls.

close up of JOSH from behind taking off his guitar and jacket helped by one of the girls.

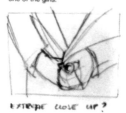

EXTREME CLOSE UP?

(17)

■
(01–16) Video images mixing archive and custom-created footage
(17–18) Process notes on recreating Ringo as the DJ

SHOT 2_DJ

BACKGROUND

ACTION

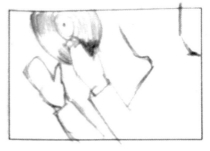

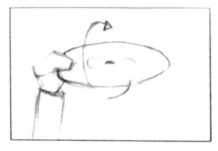

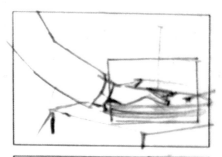

close up of JOSH DJ flipping discs

close up of JOSH DJ flipping discs

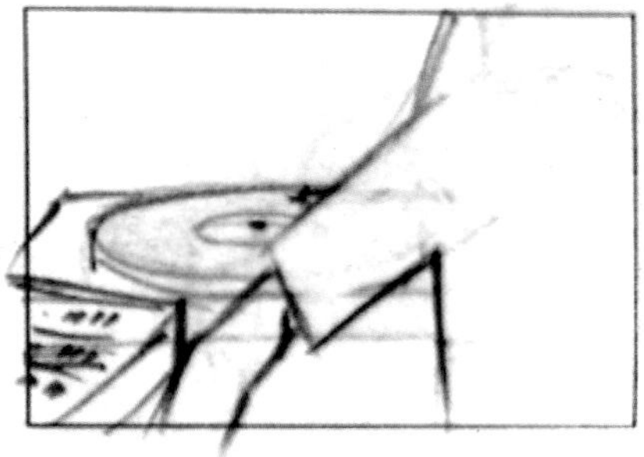

extreme and medium close up of JOSH spinning

CAMERA ANGLES
From Josh LEFT and Front looking slightly up and straight.

CAMERA ANGLES
From RIGHT looking slightly up and straight.

CAMERA ANGLES
From Josh LEFT, RIGHT and Front looking slightly up and straight.

FROM BEHIND

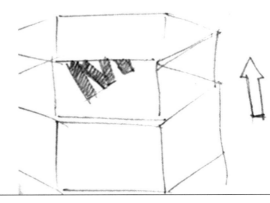

Adam Levite AKA Associates in Science / Bessy & Combe / Brand New School / Ben Dawkins / Martin de Thurah / Chris Milk / Hideaki Motoki / Muto Musashi / ne-o / Pleix / Jonas Odell / +cruz / Ramon & Pedro / Vernie Yeung / Woof Wan-Bau

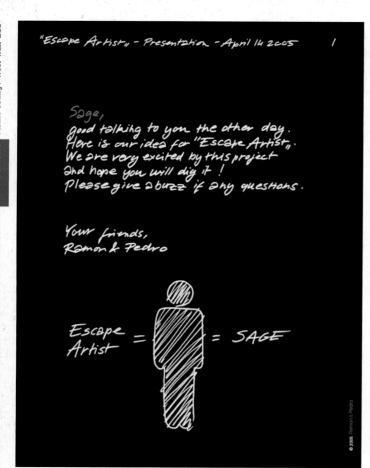

"Escape Artist" - Presentation - April 14 2005   1

Sage,
good talking to you the other day.
Here is our idea for "Escape Artist".
We are very excited by this project
and hope you will dig it!
Please give a buzz if any questions.

Your friends,
Ramon & Pedro

Escape
Artist = [icon] = SAGE

© 2005 Ramon & Pedro

(01)

"Escape Artist" - Presentation - April 14 2005   2

Open on a gritty underground NYC club. Sage Francis
is performing (here Sage wears whatever he wants, the
crazier, the better (we like the wig look)). Sage delivers
the intro of the song in front of a tight crowd. A couple
of cutaways shots single out Frank in the audience.
He is an undercover cop kinda guy. He is 35, wears a
goatie, a long black leather jacket and carries a walkie
talkie. He is clearly out of place and anxiously looks around.
Frank pushes annoyed peops around as he makes his way
to the bathroom.
Cut to a shot of the bathroom door. On the door, the
traditional black & white icon of a man, hangs half cover
with graffiti. Frank opens the door and enters in a rush.
As the door closes, the iconic man has vanished from the
sign. Cut to Sage on stage who raps for the first
time: "Escape Artist" (0:28").

© 2005 Ramon & Pedro

(02)

 ESCAPE ARTIST
▶ **SAGE FRANCIS**

Escape Artist illustrates Ramon & Pedro's
unselfconscious DIY esthetic. A reimagining of
a gritty 1970s cop show with a dash of mograph
madness in the shape of the universal icon of man
being pursued through New York's mean streets.

"A music promo for Sage Francis through Epitaph Records.
This was our only single bid presentation at the time,"
say the directors. "The story has it that Sage was given
a bunch of reels, he liked ours and we got the job. We
tried to steer away from a magician's act, so 'icon man'
trying to escape a very intense undercover cop (Sage)
was born. Twenty-four hours of straight shooting with
heavy rain made for a particularly demanding shoot.
The highlight was definitely our blinded skateboarding
icon man ollieing steps in The Village." >>>

● **SLATE**

STYLE: **LIVE ACTION WITH ANIMATION**
DISTINGUISHING FEATURE: **LO-FI/ANIMATED SILHOUETTE**
PROCESS: **DV CAMERA, SIMPLE ANIMATION**
VIDEO FOR ALBUM: *A HEALTHY DISTRUST*, SAGE FRANCIS

146

Frank comes out of the bathroom. He pounds on the door and storms out of the club. Outside, it's a busy night in NYC. Throughout the video, we cut back to Sage rapping on stage (these shots feel raw and unstaged). Cut to outside, Frank is franticly looking around. Suddenly accross the sheet a human scale icon man starts running (the icon man is an actor in a costume, please look at our visual references). Immediatly Frank chases him. This is when the track first kicks in : "In an effort to make 'em all see ▓▓▓▓ ..., (1:00").

The pursuit is fast and furious. We are in the East Village, and a big crowd is out. Frank pushes by-passers out of his way. The editing is quick cut, supporting the pace of Sage's rap. Because our fugitive (icon man) is entirely black, he tends to blend in the night, and quickly, Frank looses him. Frank stops in front of a 1$ pizzeria. He breathes heavily. Next to him, in the window of the restaurant, we reveal a wanted poster. The wanted's picture is our icon man. Cut to a close up of Frank scanning the crowd. Nothing. We cut back to the wanted poster and realize that icon man's picture is missing.

(03)

Icon man emerges out of darkness and starts sprinting again. Frank rushes after him. Icon man jumps over a Tompkins square gate, shortly followed by Frank. In the park, both man slalom through trees, jump over benches and knock trash cans down. Frank looses ground and icon man escapes again. Frank is catching his breath. On a fence, a metal plate state that: No littering, No unleashed dogs and no radio playing are allowed. We reveal a painted sign on the floor by Frank's feet : it's an icon of a skateboard with a red cross over it. We cut to Frank's sweaty face who is turning on himself in hope of finding his fugitive. Cut back to the sign on the floor. The skateboard is gone from underneath the red cross.

(04)

(05)

(07)

(09)

(11)

(06)

(08)

(10)

From behind a tree, icon man reappears on a skateboard. He is going full speed and ollies his way out of the park. Frank starts running again. This time he knows that he can't compete and dives in front of a cab. He enters in the back and orders the driver to follow icon man. A crazy car/skate chase scene on Houston St. unfolds. Frank is sticking his head out. Icon man barely clears a red light but the cab has to stop. Frank has lost him again, he is furious and decides to leave the stationery cab. He starts running again through traffic. He is mad and randomly changes direction. Suddenly, he sees an abandoned skateboard across the street, at the base of a traffic light. He knows it belongs to his man. He looks around and then back at the walk, don't walk sign. He is starting to understand... Close up of the led screen; the icon man crossing the street is lit (walk). It starts flashing and then the red light of the stop hand (don't walk) lights up. Simultaneously, behind the sign, a dark silhouette lights up. It's icon man with small light bulbs attached to him.

Icon man starts sprinting again. Frank is right behind him. Because icon man is lit, he can't really vanish anywhere. The chase is at it's climax. Cut to Sage in the club as he raps the outro: "Escape Artist" (3:15"). Both characters avoid cars and zig zag in the middle of the crowd. The sample of a man out of breath in the track (3:20") matches perfectly when we cut to Frank breathing heavily while sprinting. As icon man hits a wall with his leg, a couple of light bulbs break. This symbolizes that he is hurt and he starts limping. On his next turn, he hits a pole with his shoulder; again three light bulbs burst. He is now holding his arm. Icon man is loosing ground, and getting desperate. Finally, he jumps blindly to cross a smaller street. Out of nowhere, a car hits icon man at full speed.
Icon man is laying on the ground immobile. A couple of close up on the light bulbs show that they are fading and flickering. They finally die completely. We cut to an overhead shot of the accident. Icon man is laying in front of the car as Frank orders people to keep away. We cross fade to the same scene, a bigger crowd is gathered and the flashing lights of an ambulance are leaving. A silhouette of icon man is drawn with chalk on the pavement. (matching the lyrics: I am in two places at once) (3:30").
Fade to block.

© 2005 Ramon & Pedro

Cut to a cemetery at night. Artificial smoke is floating like in old B series horror flicks (think "Evil Dead"). We get closer to a tomb as an arm breaks through the ground from under. We witness icon man digging himself out from his grave (matching the lyrics: I am just trying to get away) (3:38). He takes a couple of steps and brushes the mud off of him. He looks up and, right in front of him, an icon woman is aiming a gun at him. She pulls the trigger. Icon man falls to the ground again. We cut back to Sage on stage delivering the last lines: I'll never fall in love with you... (4:02"). Shot of Slug coming onto stage: "Make some noise for Sage Francis y'all". Fade to black.

THE LOOK:

Because of budget reasons, we will shoot the piece on video. What that allows us to do is use multiple cameras which will give great coverage to the chosen scene (and allow kick ass editing). The video footage will then be turned to black & white and a lot of grain will be added. The final result should feel "dirty & gritty" as if shot on 8mm, a look that we love...

(03)   (04)

⏸ (01–04) Video treatment

(01)

■ INSIDE & OUT
▶ FEIST

Ramon & Pedro: "Music promo shot for Feist. We love still photography and negatives. The idea was to turn negative pictures to life and make the negative and the positive co-exist. This was shot on Super 16 in Manhattan and around NYC. It was amazing to collaborate with such a great artist."

A beautifully-wrought stylistic piece featuring lovely photo-negative shots and developing picture effects.

(02)

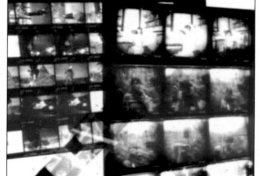

(03)

● SLATE

STYLE: LIVE ACTION
DISTINGUISHING FEATURE:
COSTUMED *TETRIS* CHARACTER
PROCESS: DV CAMERA
VIDEO FOR ALBUM: *KICKING THE NATIONAL HABIT*, GRAND NATIONAL

(04)

I LOST MY GRAVITY
DIESEL DREAMS

"Yet another commissioned film from agency KesselsKramer, for Diesel. They had created a print campaign on the theme of daydreaming: A series of people asleep during the day wearing Diesel clothes. A different pic from the campaign was given to 30 filmmakers over the globe. Ours was of a man sleeping on an escalator. The shoot happened Guerilla-style in a NYC subway a week after they had banned all use of cameras in the Metro."

A young man reads *2001*, setting him on his own personal space journey through the New York Metro. He falls asleep, then floats down the escalator, tumbling slowly and evocatively.

[01–03] The photo-negative given by R&P to Feist
[04] Free-floating underground, *2001* meets the New York Metro

VERNIE YEUNG

"Every project is different, but obviously for music videos, the track itself is the starting point," states Hong Kong-born, London-based motion-geometrist, Vernie Yeung. "I normally listen to the track repeatedly before I go to bed and fall asleep listening to it. Most of the time, I get an idea the next day. I find it very different with commercials: First of all, they have very specific briefs, you can't really go too far, whereas the music videos I've done have had a lot of freedom."

Take the revolutions of a TP_Won turntable and the scrolling landscapes of Faultline's *Biting Tongues* video, the sheared cityscapes of Supathugz' *City Soul* promo, and the searing, shimmering curves of the video for Kylie's *I Believe in You*, and you get a motion map of Vernie Yeung's directorial past. Extrapolate these lines, angles, and arrangement of forms, and one may get a glimpse into the future of music video.

Yeung landed quickly on the prestigious roster of London's RSA Black Dog Films, but his break came when he spotted a note from visionary music video commissioner Dilly Gent—who works closely on, and coordinates, Radiohead's moving image promotion—while studying for an MA at Central St Martins College of Art and Design. "At the time, she was looking for new work for Radiohead.tv [their experimental online TV channel]. I sent her my reel, even though I'd already missed the deadline. They used two of my films, *Chicken Bomb* and *Skyscape*."

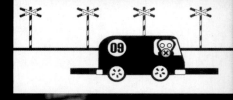

Out of these two films—the first being a stark black-and-white vector character animation, the second, a proto-Faultline clip sporting turquoise negative shapes and an upside-down cityscape—we can discern Yeung's parallel directing styles. One focuses on the character of an individual, the other on the character of the environment—most notably of the urban. The personal work such as *Chicken Bomb* appears quite anarchic and starkly simple, very different from Yeung's more technicolor commissioned music video and commercial film work.

"I find it hard to describe my own style. I wish I could erase my memory and watch all my work like I have never seen it before" VERNIE YEUNG

"It wasn't intentional," he explains. "But I do like propaganda stuff. I used to live in Camden, almost right above the station, and I had to do an instructional manual for a college project. *Chicken Bomb* was meant to be a small book, but I made the graphics move instead, because I was too lazy to print... To be honest, I didn't really think much of it after I did it, as it only took a couple of days, but it turned out to be one of my most well-received videos. *Robot Lover* is a video for a singer called Jam Lamb in Hong Kong, which contains the same character. I got the track while I was doing *Chicken Bomb*, so I used it for the video."

Compared to many other directors, Yeung's work appears more ad hoc. The way he shapes his work comes from spontaneous, instinctive decisions. "*Biting Tongues* is basically about sex," he elaborates. "The video is inspired by the journey of lovemaking, when the journey is over, the lift finally reaches its climax. I was going to create a tunnel, but at the time I thought it was too obvious, so I used a lift. I got loads of stock footage from Getty Images and compiled them together. What I couldn't find, I shot myself."

Biting Tongues is predominantly made up of a nighttime cityscape (a Yeung trope) seemingly scrolling endlessly upward. It's reminiscent of a video game arcade machine scroller. Towerblocks and high rises move by with their lights responding rhythmically to the music, with whites, greens, browns, pinks, and yellows. Striped office blocks become large-scale music equalizers. Buttresses and architectural detailing make faces. Neon-animated signs glare out like eyes. Zooming car headlights mirrored from the center of the screen remind me of the spaceship formations I used to battle in my childhood while playing *Galaxians* on the arcade game in the pub. This is all stuff that taps into the subconscious associations of modern living; of moving through space; of navigating geometries.

Yeung himself is unusual in that he appears to cross between two different directorial territories easily, producing work in both London and Hong Kong.

"Working in Hong Kong is completely different to London. I am glad I have the opportunity to work in both places. Most people in Hong Kong think the UK market is more open, but I think it depends. The idea I had for the Edison video was quite risky, because I wasn't 100 percent sure how it would come out, and I didn't have any reference or test. It was all based on trust and, of course, a good motion control turntable. Nobody knew exactly what I was doing on set. Everything is real in the video. But Edison was still very open about it. And it worked out really well."

The director is translating his acute angles and obtuse style to live action as his confidence develops. "My first performance video was for one of the greatest performers," he explains, referring to his 2005 video for Kylie. "Because she was so good, it made things a lot easier for me. The post-production for Kylie was done at The Mill, but the set is real, a lot of things you see were done in camera. It was very worrying in the beginning, because when I wrote the treatment, no one knew how we could actually build that sphere. Our art director, Chris Oddy, did an amazing job building a six meter-high sphere with 36 stilts, all dressed with fiber optics. The lighting was programmed by UVA. It was definitely a great teamwork experience."

Yeung is quickly learning which equations obtain the best results. Points and planes are being refined, and the rough edges of early spec videos and short films are being polished and precisely configured.

"I find it hard to describe my own style," concludes Yeung. "I wish I could erase my memory and watch all my work like I have never seen it before." >>>

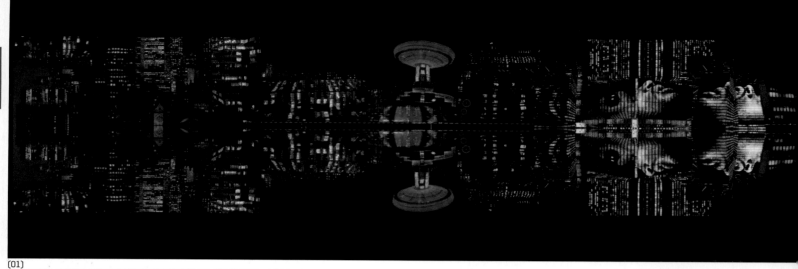

[01]

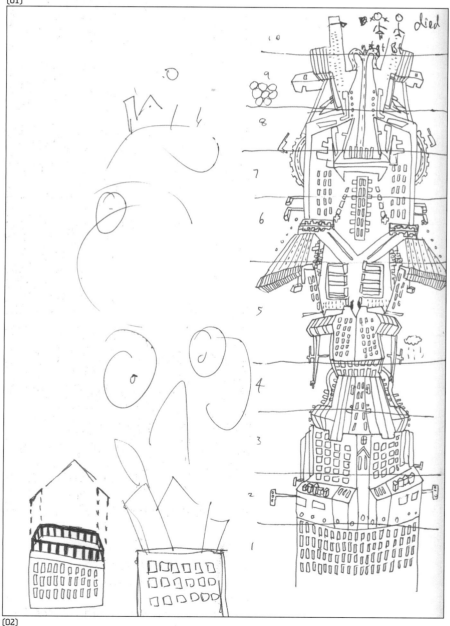

[02]

BITING TONGUES
▶ FAULTLINE

"*Biting Tongues* turned out almost exactly how it was planned, but hopefully the best is yet to come," says the director.

Yeung makes a cityscape come literally to life, as the façades of city streets scroll on and on in a mirror configuration down the screen, real-world lights and shapes taking the place of video game sprites. These photographic textures become abstracted and artificial, mutating into faces, and cyberpunk spinning tops, culminating in an ominous Eye of Sauron-style optic, blazing wildly in the center of blocks and blocks of towers. >>>

● SLATE

STYLE: GRAPHIC
DISTINGUISHING FEATURE:
CONTINUOUS SCROLLING,
MIRRORED ELEMENT
PROCESS: HEAVILY COMPOSITED
DV CAMERA FOOTAGE
VIDEO FOR ALBUM: *YOUR LOVE
MEANS EVERYTHING*, FAULTLINE

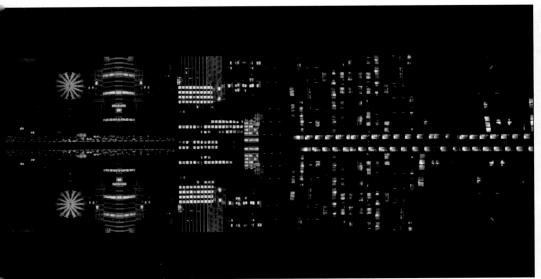

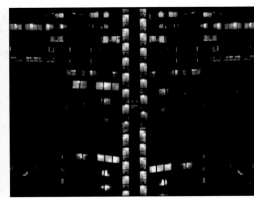

[04]

[05]

[06]

[07]

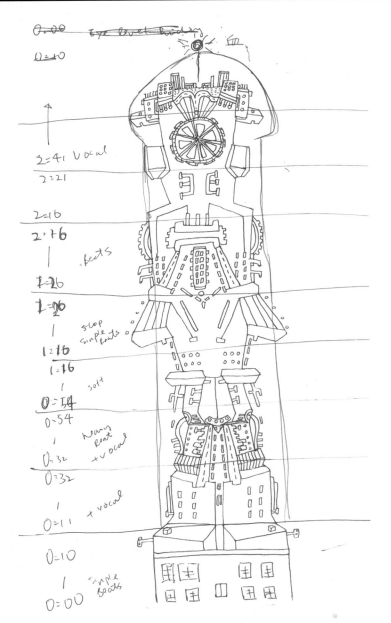

[03]

II

[01] Full scrolling cityscape
[02–03] Developing the tower of imagery through sketches
[04–07] Lights from high rise office blocks pulse in time with the track

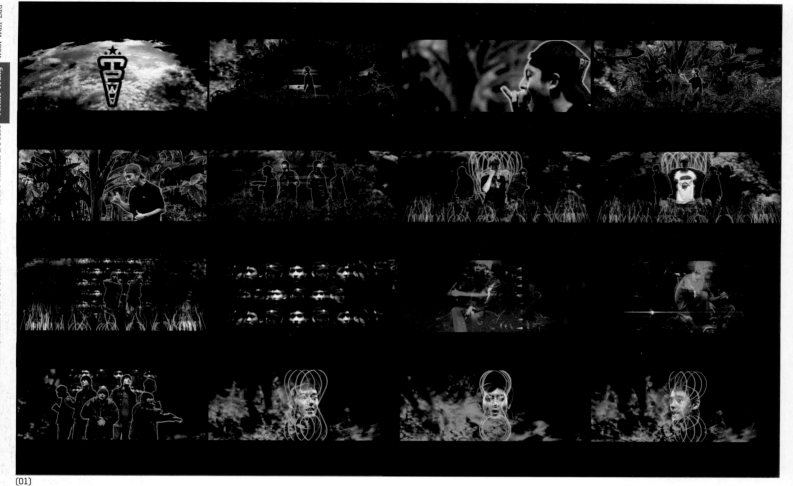

(01)

■ TP_WON
▶ EDISON

PRODUCED BY NIGO/APE SOUND

A performance video reduced to a rotating central column, with a rapper and spinning island of flora and fauna as the central focus—everything is literally rooted around this performance. Virtual wireframes, and replicated images of the vocalist, are overlaid in a radial around the center, with hints of cel-shaded outlining.

 SLATE

STYLE: COMPOSITED PERFORMANCE
DISTINGUISHING EFFECT: MOTION CONTROL TURNTABLE
PROCESS: ASSEMBLED VIDEO ELEMENTS
VIDEO FOR ALBUM: *THE 144 HOUR PROJECT*, EDISON

[02]

[03]

[04]

[05]

[06]

[07]

[08]

that are

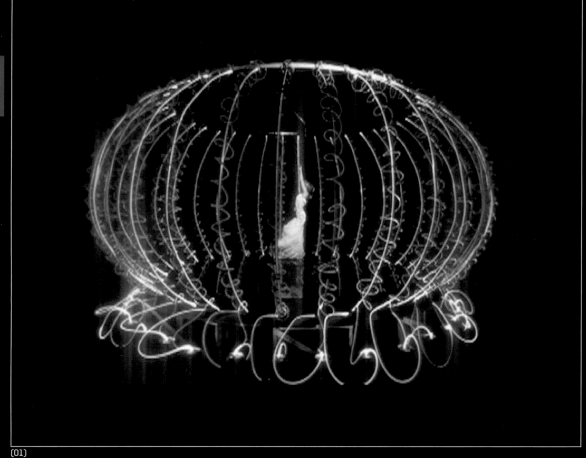

(03)

(04)

(05)

(06)

(01)

(02)

■ I BELIEVE IN YOU

► KYLIE

Yeung says, "The biggest challenge for the Kylie video wasn't filming Kylie, but was to produce the giant spinning illuminated cage which rotated in time with the music. I always wondered what it was like inside a mirrorball. If anything lived inside a mirrorball, I felt it should be Kylie, so this was the initial starting point for the video.

"The idea itself was very simple and straightforward, but I wanted it to be created with live footage rather than using CG because I wanted to really make it emphasize her performance on her own inside this space. All the cameras and lighting were outside the confines of this cage, so that as Kylie was performing, she was only aware of the cage, not the cameras or their positions, adding a more dreamy edge to her performance."

● SLATE

STYLE: **PERFORMANCE**
DISTINGUISHING FEATURE:
CAGED, REVOLVING STAGE
PROCESS: **POSTPRODUCTION AT THE MILL OF SET VIDEO, WITH LIGHTING EFFECTS BY UVA**
VIDEO FOR ALBUM:
ULTIMATE KYLIE, KYLIE

[01–06] Disco meets chilled-out Tesla coil

(01)

(02)

(03)

(04)

(05)

(06)

(07)

(08)

■ CITY SOUL

▶ SUPATHUG2

"I don't really have a top five videos," comments Yeung. "But when I was a student, a few people inspired me a lot: John Smith, Rybczynski Zbigniew, and Oskar Fischinger."

You can see this inspiration in the formalism of experiments, such as this early video, an exploratory use of the screen mirroring device that was so powerfully used in the later Faultline work. This video is more organic, seeing Yeung toying with physiognomy, as the shadow of a human face takes center stage, and lights from nighttime roads and urban vistas are superimposed over it. Dots pulse over pressure points in the face: Data and technology making a psychic impression. ■

❚❚

[01–08] Technological imprints on a face

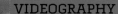

WOOF WAN-BAU

Adam Levite AKA Associates in Science / Bessy & Combe / Brand New School / Ben Dawkins / Martin de Thurah / Chris Milk / Hideaki Motoki / Muto Musashi / ne-o / Pleix / Jonas Odell / +cruz / Ramon & Pedro / Vernie Yeung

VIDEOGRAPHY

WHISTLE AND A PRAYER,	COLDCUT
CUTS ACROSS THE LAND,	THE DUKE SPIRIT
17,	YOURCODENAMEIS:MILO
MY ANGEL ROCKS BACK & FORTH,	FOUR TET
WANNA BE THAT WAY,	IKARA COLT

Woof Wan-Bau is the personae director Joji Koyama inhabits when he's directing music video. Both Koyama and Wan-Bau are equally, and refreshingly, outspoken. This split is the first step in the process of how this particular director creates his work: It would be too simplistic to say Koyama is the yin to Wan-Bau's yang, even if the triple bark translation of his pseudonym is something of a warning. More accurately, they are balance and counterbalance. They both produce and overcome one another, and the end result is a range of styles deliberately set to unbalance. I don't think it would be too much of a stretch to see this as a deliberate philosophical stance, or an attempt to create one.

Although Koyama moved as a child from Japan to the UK (he is London-based), we can play a game (reflecting the director's own Far-Eastern whimsy) of seeing his moving image universe inflected through the qualities of the Asian philosophy *wu hsing*, composed of: The movements of the stars; the workings of the body; the nature of foods; the qualities of music; the ethical qualities of humans; the progress of time; the operations of government; and the nature of historical change.

> "I don't get very excited with videos that 'show off' an effect or technique... I guess I just think it's boring when all you're left with is, 'Wow, how did they do that?'" WOOF WAN-BAU

THE MOVEMENTS OF THE STARS

"It's hard for me to say, as I don't know what it was like before, say in the 1980s for example," Woof Wan-Bau says in regard to the current state of the music video industry. "I do know that, generally speaking, budgets have gone down, and record companies seem much more reluctant to take risks. It all seems incredibly 'professional,' which I think is a great shame. It annoys me sometimes when I'm working with a group of people who, as far as I can tell, have been drilled with a kind of professionalism that I can't stand—everything has to be done in a certain way—and they look at me as though I've just murdered someone if I veer away from that. I definitely think people need to loosen up a bit, and have a bit more fun, forget about the rote systems that they've been trained with and be on their toes a little more."

We can reduce this to: Take inspiration from playing with the form. Unlearn systems to create something new. Don't buy into corporate taste.

THE WORKINGS OF THE BODY

"I'm currently in preproduction for two new short film projects. I've been trying to divide things up a little bit in terms of my own films. I don't use my Woof Wan-Bau moniker with the films, because I make music videos as Woof Wan-Bau, which is very different from making short films. It's not a hierarchical thing, they're just different. It's just a way to try and keep the two sides of what I do separate. In the end, especially nowadays, I don't think it's ever possible to have control over how and where things get seen, so the least I can do is try and set up some sort of divide, even if it's a little superficial."

Even if viewed as an artificial divide, if this demarcation helps the creative process, then it can only be a good thing. It is in service to the art. If it becomes a fad, a pose, like the suspiciously popular turn-of-the-century trend of individuals clustering into collectives, then it becomes mere obfuscation.

THE NATURE OF FOODS

The visual serves the aural in music video. But at its best, the two inform each other to create a new dynamic. Sometimes, it is easier to make a flavorsome dish if you are not destroying your favorite foods to do so.

"I once sat down and wrote out a wish list of music I'd like to make videos for. I quickly realized that none of the musicians on my list would ever have the money to make a video. But actually, I now feel it's more fun to take a track I really don't like and do something with it—if they let me—because pasting on images to music I really love is, strangely, not that appealing."

THE QUALITIES OF MUSIC

"Working with a musician directly on a film is obviously very different—the dynamics are switched around—because I'm approaching the musicians, rather than them or a record company approaching me."

Working as Koyama, the elements are more fluid. For many directors, music video direction is a way to learn the craft and the technical skills of direction, which they can then apply to their more self-derived visions. This was the case with Koyama's UK Channel 4 commissioned short film, *Watermelon Love*.

"For *Watermelon Love*, I worked with Isambard Khroustaliov, who is one half of electronic group Icarus, along with singer-songwriter Tujiko Noriko. It's an entirely collaborative process, especially as I'm very particular about how sound is used in a film. I'll actually be there in the studio, working closely with them as I did with the animators. I don't like the idea of just taking a piece of music and slapping it onto a film, it has to be in some way integral to it. Khroustaliov has just agreed to do the music and sound for my two new short films, which I'm really happy about, because we've developed a real understanding of how we can work together." >>>

THE ETHICAL QUALITIES OF HUMANS

Having a personal connection with the artist helps immensely. It is easy to see why a director can work on a track he has no real passion for when many music artists have such a disconnect, such a lack of interest, in their visual presentation. When you get the enlightened opposite, then the collaboration can reap dividends. The unusual esthetic and poeticism of Four Tet's *My Angel Rocks Back & Forth* is a direct result of this artistic response.

"Making a video for Kieran [Hebden, a.k.a. Four Tet] always seems a lot more informal and loose—which is better for me, because I like to keep things open wherever it's possible," explains Wan-Bau. "It was probably dumb to choose an eight-minute track, but I thought it had these distinct sections in the music that you usually don't get in music videos, so I thought I could do something with different 'acts.' I told Kieran that I'd do it on one condition—he had to be in it. I'd always noticed how Kieran could produce these incredible facial expressions and I thought it would be great to catch that on screen. I'm a big fan of Chinese Opera and Kabuki, not so much for its dialog or plot, but for its intense mannerisms. I wanted to try and create a similar out-of-this-world atmosphere in the video. We were restricted by budget and time so I ended up playing the panda myself."

THE PROGRESS OF TIME

The directorial streams of Koyama and Wan-Bau currently run side by side: "At the moment, I'm in preproduction for two short films. One of them is called *From Nose to Mouth*, which is funded by the Arts Council and is largely live-action, and the other one, *Flicker*, is fully animated, 2D-drawn animation."

THE OPERATIONS OF GOVERNMENT

Watermelon Love is a lushly animated short that segues between curvaceous stylized lines and super-saturated colors, to photorealistic CG. But it also illustrates how music video, with all its restrictions as a form, can also be liberating compared to one that has to be produced for, and within, the confines of delivery for a traditional broadcast channel.

"My first animated short film, and my first time directing 3D CG animators. The process of getting this made was a little frustrating because it was partly funded by TV, with a heavy development policy that I found excruciatingly condescending. I had to go to these aggressive scriptwriting workshops that made me want to vomit. But I didn't let that spoil what for me was a chance to finally make a short film of my own, even though I look at it as something that came about out of circumstance. It was made for TV, and I made it with that audience in mind—as something that suddenly came on after the news. It has a vaguely interactive theme to it. The film is totally non-interactive, but I guess that was the point. I was interested in the relationship between desire and fantasy, or how a simulated fantasy could teach you how and what to desire. I was wondering whether there was some sort of erotic investment in the process of configuring a desire to fit into a logic."

THE NATURE OF HISTORICAL CHANGE

"Every video I've done has been, in one way or another, a technical challenge for me, because I'm not very technically minded—technique is probably the last thing on my mind when I write a treatment. That's why I usually panic briefly when a video gets confirmed. But collaborating with people who are technical is something I enjoy a lot."

With his series of music promos so far, Koyama/Wan-Bau has shown a stylistic verve, and willingness to embrace narrative concepts rather than simple technical pose. The next short films from the two-headed director will decide whether his bite is worse than his bark.

(01)

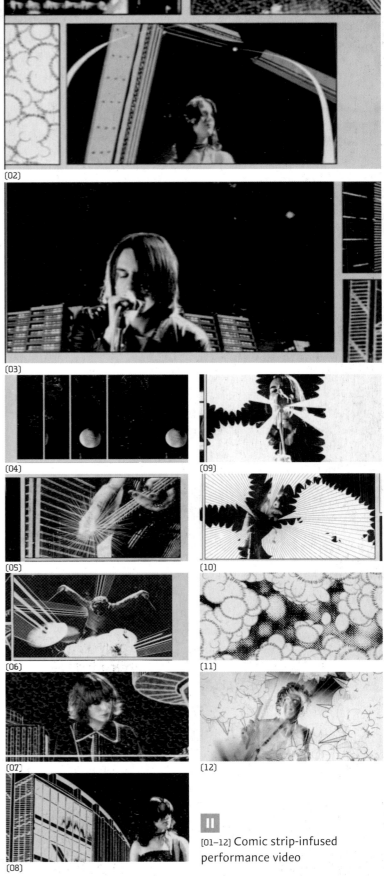

(02)

(03)

(04)

(05)

(06)

(07)

(08)

(09)

(10)

(11)

(12)

WANNA BE THAT WAY
▶ IKARA COLT

This video for Ikara Colt manages to present the anarchy and vibrancy of the band's sound through framing it in a manga-like context. Dynamic lines vibrate from guitars, while the next comic-strip panel sees soundwaves resonating through a cosmos that will have you seeing stars. Using halftone dots, line textures, and high-contrast and inverted black-and-white photography, this influential music video brings a fanzine-style comic book to life.

The director explains: "I was quite keen at the time to mess around with motion graphics and animated motifs, so when this track came along, I thought it fitted the bill. I love the graphic language of Japanese comics. One of the interesting things about them is that a lot of the templates, textures, and background materials are all readily available for anyone to use. I used to draw comics myself, so I had a whole pile of these ready-made templates filed away.

"It was a ridiculously tight schedule. We worked straight through Christmas and New Year. I learned a lot from this video, in that it was really the first time I'd worked with a small team of animators—a way of working that was still very foreign to me. It's quite polished, but I think it's one of my more boring videos." >>>

● SLATE

STYLE: PERFORMANCE, GREEN SCREEN COMPOSITES
DISTINGUISHING FEATURE: COMIC-BOOK FRAMING
PROCESS: FILMED BAND PERFORMANCE FRAMED INSIDE MANGA AND COMIC-BOOK REFERENCES USING PRE-MADE TEMPLATES AND CLIP ART
VIDEO FOR ALBUM: *MODERN APPRENTICE*, IKARA COLT

[01–12] Comic strip-infused performance video

(01)

(02)

(03)

(04)

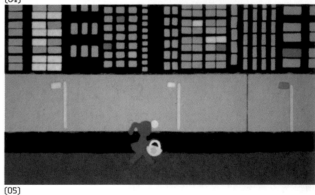

(05)

■ WHISTLE AND A PRAYER
▶ COLDCUT

"Coldcut wanted to have the video animated with Fuzzy Felt. When I found out what Fuzzy Felt was, I liked the idea of using these things without me having to design or make any of the material.
I didn't want it to be a 'technique' video. I don't get very excited with videos that 'show off' an effect or technique... I guess I just think it's boring when all you're left with is, 'Wow, how did they do that?'

"I enjoyed this one a lot because they really let me get on with it and weren't concerned at all if the ideas evolved. It involved a tiny team of two; myself and Dean Koonjul. *Whistle and a Prayer* is a simple stop-motion animated adventure of a girl strolling and scrolling down a 2D city road of exploding cars and other dangerous obstacles. The childlike associations of the Fuzzy Felt animation rub up against a more adult world of peril and riskiness." >>>

● SLATE

STYLE: **STOP MOTION ANIMATION**
DISTINGUISHING FEATURE: **LO-FI FUZZY FELT**
PROCESS: **STOP MOTION USING FUZZY
FELT KIT AND DV CAMERA**
VIDEO FOR ALBUM: ***SOUND MIRRORS*, COLDCUT**

[01–10] Stop-motion animation

(06)

(07)

(09)

(08)

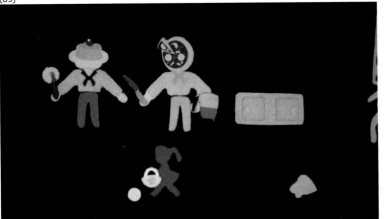

(10)

● SLATE

STYLE: PERFORMANCE, GREEN SCREEN COMPOSITES
DISTINGUISHING FEATURE: GEORGES MÉLIÈS-
STYLE VISUAL EFFECT COMPOSITES
PROCESS: VIDEO AGAINST GREEN SCREEN, WITH ANIMATION
ELEMENTS COMPOSITED WITH MINIMAL SET ELEMENTS
VIDEO FOR ALBUM: *CUTS ACROSS THE LAND*, DUKE SPIRIT

■ CUTS ACROSS THE LAND
▶ THE DUKE SPIRIT

"This one was always going to be tricky to pull off
with the budget—which was low—but I thought, 'What
the hell?' I originally wanted to build sets and shoot
everything in camera, but it just wasn't going to be
possible, so I settled for building the hair for real, but
compositing the scenes," explains Wan-Bau. "It's always
difficult to do something fun when the band are in it, so
I tried to make the most of the characters in the band."

This is like the Ikara Colt video, in that a performance
video is camouflaged beyond recognition through
a particular atmosphere and technique. Here, The
Duke Spirit are presented like a magic lantern
show. The video in its early stages is reminiscent
of Jonathan Dayton and Valerie Faris's seminal
Smashing Pumpkins video for *Tonight, Tonight*.
But as elements such as the lighthouse, bubble car
with backdrop projection, and planets held on rods are
introduced, the Méliès-style cocktail becomes more
delirious and confusing rather than simple homage.

(01)
(02)   (07)
(03)   (08)
(04)   (09)
(05)   (10)
(06)   (11)

Ⅱ

[01–11] Composited performance video

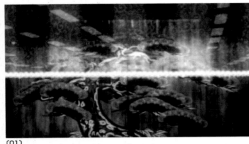

(01)

(02)

(03)

(04)

(05)

(06)

(01–02)

MY ANGEL ROCKS BACK & FORTH
FOUR TET

"My first attempt at animation, this was a real test, in that I just threw myself into it, to see if I could make the kind of scenes and moods that I'd always fantasized about making in animation. The idea was, in part, dictated by the severe technical limitations, and although all the geeks will say it looks a bit amateurish, when we finished it, I felt that I was onto something that I could explore further."

Beautifully flawed, this animation wears imperfection with grace and an evocative period effect, like 1950s-style Japanese film (think *Suzuki Seijun*), remixed with traditional Noh drama, and contemporary spaces. With an inky painterly quality, exquisite bland and gray gradations mix 3D environments and crude 2D animation.

(03–04)

17
YOURCODENAMEIS: MILO

Chi Gong meets indoor bowls in this everyday tale of telekinesis between a female bowler and her one-eyed evil nemesis. The pink bowls have a life of their own as they are choreographed through intricate mind control by two opponents in the incongruous location of an artificial bowling green. The set-up between the mundane environment and strange goings-on draw on absurdist drama and experimental cinema in this live action music video.

"I'd been pitching a lot of live action ideas with no success," Wan-Bau remembers. "The Ikara Colt video was becoming a bit of a curse because I don't know how many times I got asked to do the same thing for other bands—and I'd end up pitching something entirely different, which inevitably they didn't want. So when this happened, it was a bit of a relief.

"A lot of 'first times' on this one: My first live-action location shoot and my first collaboration with a postproduction house. I think if I knew what I know now, I would have done things a little differently, but there's an intentional awkwardness to this video that I think comes across the way I wanted it to."

(05–06)

WATERMELON LOVE
SHORT FILM

Wan-Bau: "I was interested in the relationship between desire and fantasy, or how a simulated fantasy could 'teach' you how and what to desire. I was wondering whether there was some sort of erotic investment in the process of configuring a desire to fit into a logic. The film has had a strange and varied circulation on the Internet, festivals, and DVDs. I'm looking forward to making my next short film, which will be very different."

A seductive animation literally reshaping our notions of sex and food, through a capsule narrative tale of a mouthwatering watermelon remade into cubic form. The film riffs on the interesting pop-cultural fact that high-priced Japanese watermelons were recently being grown in box-like forms, and takes us on a more subversive food/sex analogy regarding the human need to mold our desires to fabricate something more artificially exotic. ∎

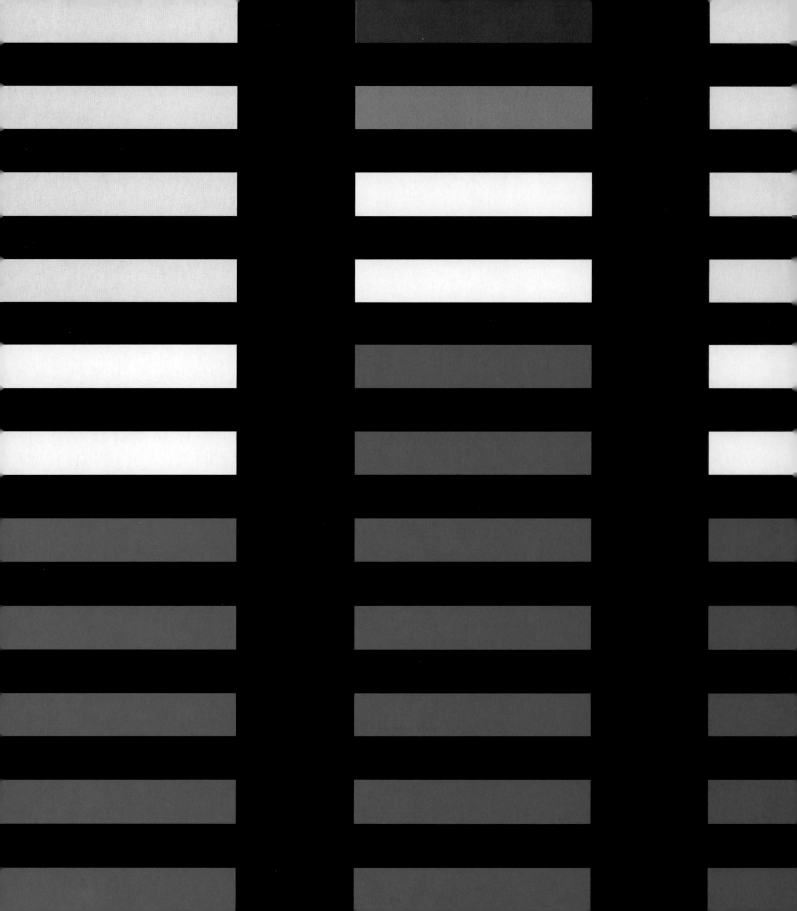

GLOSSARY

TERMS

ANIMATICS
Crudely animated 3D storyboard to aid shot framing, sequencing, and movement. Also see Previsualizations.

ANIMÉ
Japanese animation.

A&R
artist and repertoire. The A&R department is responsible for talent development and scouting within a record company.

CF
Commercial film.

CEL-SHADING
Type of animation emulating the hand shading of cells in traditional animation, often to create an outlined cartoonish look.

CG/CGI
Short for computer generated, and computer-generated imagery.

CHARA CHARA
Japanese slang for something that is too flashy in terms of style.

COMPOSITE (ALSO COMP)
A final image made up of different and separately constructed layered elements.

DRM
Digital rights management.

DV
Digital video. Also a specific digital tape format.

GREEN SCREEN
A pure green screen used to create a clean matte, to define the areas of the image that are to be transparent. Once the subject is isolated as an element, it can then be composited in a background. Green screens offer better reviews when working with digital camera equipment, as opposed to the more traditional blue screen.

HD HIGH DEFINITION
High definition video resolution is 1,080 interlaced lines or 720 progressive lines compared with 480 lines in NTSC TV systems, or 576 lines in PAL/SECAM systems.

MANGA
Japanese comic books.

MATCH-MOVING (ALSO MOTION TRACKING)
A term that refers to different ways of extracting information from video or film footage, particularly with reference to camera movement.

MATTE
Used in filmmaking to insert part of a foreground image onto a background image.

MOCAP
Motion capture, a method of capturing fluid human movement, turning it into digital information to use in animation and CG work.

MV
Music video.

ONLINE EDIT
An edit containing high-resolution imagery that is ready to master a high-quality image from.

OFFLINE EDIT
An edit containing low-resolution imagery. This is often made to save disk space, offering just enough resolution to roughly edit the footage together; as extraneous footage takes up valuable hard disk space.

PIKARI
Japanese slang meaning to rip off, imitate, or steal.

PREVIS (SOMETIMES PREVIZ)
Previsualization. Animated storyboards, and initial renders of effects shots are essential in planning how a scene is to be composited and fully realized.

PROMO
Promotional video. Mainly English usage.

RENDER
A depiction of a digital effect must be rendered using appropriate animation or imaging software. Renders can be complete, or in various stages of process. Early renders, for example, may be comprised of less polygons, and detailing such as texture maps and lighting.

SPEC VIDEO
Speculative video, used to present and showcase a particular idea of the director, or use as a calling card.

SPECIAL EFFECTS (SFX)
On-set pyrotechnics and physical effects.

SOFTWARE

SPOT
A commercial film or advertisement spot, usually 30 to 60 seconds in length.

SUPER-DEFORMED
A highly exaggerated style of drawn character, to be found in animé or manga. This style, sometimes called "chibi," presents "cute" representations of characters with stubby limbs and oversized heads.

TELECINE
The process of transferring film to video format.

TEST PIECE
A piece of work completed to showcase or test the viability of a style or technique.

3DS MAX
Customizable, scaleable 3D animation, modeling, and rendering solution.
www.autodesk.com

AFTER EFFECTS
Adobe's pioneering video compositing software.
www.adobe.com

AVID
A long-standing video software and hardware manufacturer provding digital non-linear media creation (NLE) tools.
www.avid.com

COMBUSTION
Autodesk's comprehensive desktop motion graphics, compositing, and visual effects solution.
www.autodesk.com

FINAL CUT PRO
Apple's next-generation desktop digital video software. www.apple.com/finalcutstudio/finalcutpro/

FLAME
Industry-leading real-time visual effects design and compositing system.
www.autodesk.com

FLASH
Vector-graphics animation standard for creating and viewing animations (particularly for, but not limited to, online use).
www.adobe.com

INFERNO
Design system for high-resolution visual effects.
www.autodesk.com

LIGHTWAVE 3D
3D animation production pipeline, comprising modeling tools and character animation.
www.newtek.com

MATCHMOVER
3D movement tracking software.
www.realviz.com

MAYA
Integrated 3D modeling, animation, effects, and rendering solution.
www.alias.com

MENTAL RAY
Rendering solution, streamlines the output of photorealistic to stylized visualizations.

PHOTOSHOP
Adobe's groundbreaking still image manipulation software.
www.adobe.com

PREMIERE
Adobe's pioneering desktop digital video software.
www.adobe.com

XSI
A high-end 3D graphics application.
www.softimage.com

INDEX

INDEX

BIBLIOGRAPHY

Building Sci-Fi Moviescapes,
Matt Hanson (RotoVision, 2005)

www.eternalgaze.net

Motion Blur: Graphic Moving Imagemakers,
Matt Hanson & Shane Walter (Lawrence King, 2004)

www.mvdbase.com

www.mvwire.com

On Air: The Visual Messages and Global Languages of MTV,
R. Klanten & C. Jofré & B. Meyer & S. Lovell (Die Gestalten Verlag, 2005)

Res magazine
www.res.com

Teaching Music Video,
Peter Fraser (British Film Institute, 2005)

The End of Celluloid: Film Futures in the Digital Age
Matt Hanson (RotoVision, 2004)

Thirty Frames Per Second: The Visionary Art of the Music Video,
Neil Feineman & Steve Reiss (Harry N. Abrams, 2000)

ACKNOWLEDGMENTS

As always, many thanks to my editor Leonie Taylor for her crucial guidance and motivational powers. Paul Farrington of Studio Tonne for illuminating the text with his design. Hamamoto Taeko for Japanese translation, and Tom Ridgway for French translation work. Many thanks to April Sankey, Chris Middleton and all at RotoVision for believing in the book and making it happen.

I am especially grateful to all the directors featured in the book, who all consented to interrogation and analysis with grace and enthusiasm. Thanks for giving your time, and especially to those providing personal notes and visual documents.

Finally, thanks to all others who were invaluable in making this book happen in some way, including:

Jennifer Amerine Heath, @radical.media
Carmen Montanez-Callen, Academy Films
Diane Chan, Chris O'Reilly, Nexus
Gustav Grass, Independent
CJ and John Hassay, Colonel Blimp
Paul McKee, Love TV
Sasha Nixon, Partizan
Daniel Siegler, Neon
And all the video commissioners and record companies responsible for keeping music video a lustrous and vibrant artform.

BIOGRAPHY

Matt Hanson is a film futurist; a writer and filmmaker described as an "international film visionary" by Screen International magazine. He founded the massively influential onedotzero digital film festival which he directed from 1996 to 2002. He now runs V.I.A. (Visual Intelligence Agency), a moving image consultancy. He has previously authored *The End of Celluloid*, and *Building Sci-Fi Moviescapes*, for RotoVision.